Jesus and Theology

Jesus and Theology

Critique of a Tradition

JENS GLEBE-MÖLLER

Translated by Thor Hall

FORTRESS PRESS MINNEAPOLIS

JESUS AND THEOLOGY
Critique of a Tradition

Original Danish edition published 1984 under the title *Jesus og teologien: Kritik af en tradition* by G. E. D. Gad, Copenhagen.

Scripture quotations unless otherwise noted are from the Revised Standard Version of the Bible, copyright 1946, 1952, and 1971 by the Division of Christian Education of the National Council of Churches.

Excerpts from Choan-Seng Song's *Third-Eye Theology* and John Francis Kavanaugh's *Following Christ in a Consumer Society* appear by permission of the publishers, Orbis Books, Maryknoll, N. Y., and Lutterworth Press, Cambridge, England.

Cover art: Woodcut by Georges Roualt, in *Passion* (Ambroise Vollard, 1939), courtesy Walker Art Center, Minneapolis.

Cover design: Mark Stratman
Interior design: Karen Buck

Library of Congress Cataloging-in-Publication Data

Glebe-Möller, Jens.
Jesus and theology: critique of a tradition.

Bibliography: p.
Includes index.
1. Jesus Christ—History of doctrines. 2. Jesus Christ—Person and offices. 3. Bible. N.T.—Criticism, interpretation, etc. 4. Spirituality. I. Title.
BT198.G53 1989 232 88-45863
ISBN 0-8006-2334-7

The paper used in this publication meets the minimum requirements of American National Standard for Information Sciences—Permanence of Paper for Printed Library Materials, ANSI Z329.48-1984. ∞™

Manufactured in the U.S.A. AF 1-2334

93 92 91 90 89 1 2 3 4 5 6 7 8 9 10

The difficulty lies
not in the new ideas,
but in escaping from the old ones,
which ramify,
for those brought up
as most of us have been,
into every corner
of our minds.

John Maynard Keynes

CONTENTS

PREFACE

The present book develops further the viewpoints in *A Political Dogmatic* (Glebe-Möller 1987), especially its Chapter 6.

Part of the material was gathered in Montreal during a period of study made possible by a stipend from Jens Nörregaard's and Hal Koch's memorial fund, to whose administration I hereby acknowledge my indebtedness. I also thank Professor Alastair McKinnon and his wife, Mildred, for all their personal kindnesses and for my introduction to Canada's philosophical and theological-ecclesiastical life.

Thanks also to my colleagues at Theologicum for many inspiring discussions and, finally, to Kirsten Hansen, who helped me finish the manuscript.

Jens Glebe-Möller

INTRODUCTION

In the fall of 1982 I published my book *A Political Dogmatic.* My intention with that book was to offer a descriptive signalment of modernity, and on that basis to sketch what in my view will be the nature of the dogmatic task in the last fifth of the twentieth century.

The book received plentiful review and commentary, especially in the churchly and theological press. These commentaries and reviews were, however, almost without exception negative. Clearly, most reviewers had no difficulty accepting my characterizations of modernity—which of course were based mainly on the American sociologist of religion Peter L. Berger, the West German philosopher and sociologist Jürgen Habermas, and through them, that is, indirectly, on Max Weber. But when it came to my treatment of dogmatics or theology, the rejection was almost unanimous. I had not expected anything else. *A Political Dogmatic* was written, after all, as an *opgör* (squaring of accounts) with two to three generations of theological culture—in Denmark, mind you! Moreover, in that book I had begun to include extensive references to texts and viewpoints from the Anglo-Saxon world, especially the United States, while as everybody knows, our homespun theological traditions in Denmark have to a considerable degree and for several reasons been more oriented toward Germany.

Chapter 6 of that book is entitled "Christology from Below."

In that chapter I attempted, again rather sketchily, to say something about how in my judgment a modern christology must appear and be approached. Unfortunately, not even that chapter found favor in the eyes of theologically well-established reviewers. I have, however, been pleased to observe that at least a few younger theologians, as well as some laypeople without formal theological schooling, have been interested in and in agreement with the book as a whole and the chapter on christology in particular. This has encouraged me to continue my considerations, even though—because of my position, which some of my critics apparently think I ought to give up!—this includes continuing to work on the fundamental problematic of the book. My colleague Theodor Jörgensen's extensive review has posed an important challenge in this regard.

One reviewer wrote that *A Political Dogmatic* is "a sort of Marxist-inspired sociology of religion," that is, something altogether different from theology. On the one hand, I must confess that I tend to take that sort of characterization rather lightly: I have learned to say with Mary Daly, "I couldn't have cared less whether what I was doing was or wasn't theology in his terms" (see below, chap. 3, sec. 2). On the other hand, it bothers me that one can so quickly dismiss the book as "not theological."

In the first place, I am oriented just as much as everybody else to certain traditional scholarly positions, to "already existing contexts of interpretation" (see below, chap. 1, sec. 4). While my philosophical basis is predominantly German, my theological orientation is English, or at least English-language based. And as I have already mentioned, my critics have very little knowledge of that tradition.

Second, I would claim that my critics have no patented rights to the label "theology." They, of course, write and think on the basis of their own interpretations of the Jesus-narratives of the New Testament, just as I do. The difference between them and me is therefore not a difference in theology, but a difference in method. They (I generalize) will read the biblical texts on the basis of (I generalize again) existential-philosophical principles; I read them along sociological lines.

But then, I must tell myself, you cannot think that you will get by these critics that easily! For the situation is this: my critics have read my book the same way they read the Bible, that is, on the basis of what I am calling here the "theological code." This refers, briefly stated, to a definitive interpretive tradition that says that God, who created the world and exists "out there" as person, from eternity and by the Holy Spirit has "begotten" the Son, Jesus Christ, who at a certain point in time, namely, at the beginning of the Christian era, "descended" to earth and there suffered death upon a cross in order that all the sins that humans have brought into the world since the beginning of creation might be "atoned for" and forgiven. But this atonement and forgiveness constitutes only the first phase. The second phase is that that same God, in the Son, will come again at the end of time and finally reestablish the original order of creation. And now, in the interval between the first and second phases, God governs and directs believers—those who believe that the Son of God has suffered death to atone for their and all humanity's sin—by the Holy Spirit, who is the third person of the Trinity.

This code is what millions and millions of people in the Western world have been raised with. (I myself am no exception.) And ever since the Europeans began their advance across the globe some five hundred years ago, Africans, Asians, and others have also learned this code.

In my view this code is "wrong": it speaks of social realities by way of "wrong" sentences (for explanation, see below, chap. 7, sec. 1). This means that there are moral consequences that are unacceptable. Stated very briefly, in formula form, the code leads to the acceptance of oppression in human society. Of course, I know very well that many of the adherents of the code through the ages have been engaged in—even at times obsessed with—the struggle against oppression, but I also know that apart from a few notable exceptions—and Karl Barth is one of the best—they have not taken as their motivation the source on which everything, after all, depends for a theologian, namely, the story of Jesus of Nazareth.

And so I do not believe in the theological code, and in this new book I try to point to alternatives to it. I utilize therefore many lengthy quotations, in an effort to introduce a new context of interpretation.

The book is structured as follows: In Chapters 1 and 2, I make an attempt at a critical discussion of the traditional foundations of christology, namely, New Testament exegesis. In Chapter 3, I sketch a few aspects of "spirituality," and in Chapter 4 some modern christologies from the world of blacks in the United States and from the third world. Chapters 5 and 6 form an interlude where I test the viewpoints from the first four chapters on two church-historical and dogmatic themes, respectively: one aspect of the christology of the early church, and some christological tendencies during the Reformation. Chapter 7 represents my "positive" attempt to draw a sketch or silhouette of a modern christology. And finally, in Chapter 8, I confront the newly sketched christology with several representative forms of "new religiosity."

At the end of the book I list the literature cited and other relevant sources discussed in the text. In some instances I have supplemented the discussion within the text with additional endnotes. The index includes the orientation of the past- and present-era scholars and writers to whom I have referred in the text.

1. Modern Exegesis

1. The Historical-Critical Method

In the Western world today, the church understood as the institutional and organizational framework of the Christian religion has only limited influence. Secularization has taken over—perhaps most clearly in Denmark and other Scandinavian welfare societies. A little Christian revival here and there, some flowering of religious interest in times of crisis—when politics and the economy do not seem to function properly, one might as well try religion—but the overall picture does not change. The Christian religion is no longer what it was prior to the breakthrough of capitalism and industrialization toward the end of the previous century: the religion of *all* the people. It must now constantly compete with other religions, with the so-called youth-religions or with various political ideologies, and in addition must respond to the general apathy among people or to the struggle for the leftover pieces of the layer cake.

The Jesus-figure is nevertheless still an essential part of Western civilization, even in Scandinavia. Those who no longer go to church and hear the minister preach about Jesus or sing hymns about him or participate in the eucharistic memory of him—they will still read Nicholas Grundtvig's hymns in Danish literature classes, go to museums, to art exhibits, or as hosts take foreign guests by the old village church. And everywhere they go, they meet the Jesus-figure. Jesus' words float around as common expressions—"no one can serve two masters," "do unto others . . . ," and many more—and now as before, books are being written about Jesus. Even books and films that make no mention of Jesus may perhaps nevertheless have something to do with him.

But where do we get the material from which both the traditional and the contemporary images of Jesus are formed? In the last analysis, from the New Testament, the oldest written narratives about him. Well then, can we not simply go to the New Testament and find out who this Jesus was—what he wanted to say—and on the basis of our reading say what ought to be said in a modern christology?

The matter, unfortunately, is not that simple! The book about Jesus is almost two thousand years old—and it is part of our modern consciousness to realize that a span of two thousand years (and much less, for that matter) creates difficulties for the understanding of a text. A historical text, we know, is written out of entirely different suppositions from our own; its "horizon," as the German philosopher Hans-Georg Gadamer expresses it (Gadamer 1965, 286; 1975, 269–70), is different from ours.

Is the task then not to describe these suppositions as exactly and comprehensively as possible, in order to find out what the New Testament authors desired to say through their text? That, at least, is what historical-critical exegesis has claimed ever since its infancy back in the seventeenth century—even though at that time it also had another aim in sight: to liberate the Bible from the church and the churchly tradition (cf. Davis 1982, 270). And if we gather together all the books and articles about the Bible which this exegesis has produced—well, then we must at the very least acknowledge that quantitatively it has come very far! It has been *historical,* first and foremost because it has wanted to get at the historical facts concerning and included in the biblical texts. And it has been *critical* for the same reason: because it has not taken the texts, as they exist, as given, or interpreted them on face value. A modern exegete, Walter Vogels, offers the following characteristic of the historical-critical method:

> [It] goes at the texts with a certain scepticism. Because of the age of the texts and the long period of their transmission, it harbors some suspicion that the texts have been corrupted. It then tries, by way of text criticism, to reconstruct the original text. In the process, it is struck by the disharmonies in the text; it discovers breaks, logical deficiencies, repetitions and other irregularities. It then tries to distinguish between various levels in the text, or to separate out different additions, as one can do with the prophetic texts, for example. From there one reaches the theory of the four traditions in the Pentateuch [the five "Books of Moses" —JG-M] and then the theory of the two sources of the synoptic gospels. One and the same tradition in the Pentateuch is sometimes divided up in small pieces. One can distinguish between several layers of it. Depending on the skills of the exegete, one can arrive at some pretty impressive reconstructions. People have even talked about the cut-'n-paste epoch to which some authors still seem to belong. In short, one studies the texts' genesis. The perspective of the historical-critical method is thus clearly diachronic. (Vogels 1980, 182f.)

2. Deficiencies in the Method

For users of the biblical texts the deficiencies of the historical-critical exegesis are obvious. Vogels claims, among other things, that the method has effected a divorce between the study of the Old Testament and the study of the New Testament, simply because the number of historical-detail studies has become so overwhelming that no one can encompass and master more than one of the Testaments. One becomes a professor of the one Testament or the other! This situation was unheard of earlier. The three first theological professors at the newly established Copenhagen University were all obligated according to the 1539 charter to lecture on Holy Scripture, and it was left up to them to decide who was to take what parts of the Old Testament or the New. We must go all the way to the middle of the nineteenth century before we encounter the first specialist (Johan Frederik Hagen was named professor of church history with Old Testament as adjunct subject in 1852), and only in our own century do the teaching chairs in Old Testament and New Testament, respectively, appear. For many hundreds of years, and read without the diachronic perspective (and without historical consciousness), the Old Testament and the New Testament corresponded to each other as prophecy and fulfillment, and both Testaments were considered immediately applicable to the readers or hearers—as can be seen, for example, in Niels Hemmingsen's large authorship (Glebe-Möller 1979).

Another consequence is that the exegetes have become, in the eyes of others and not least in their own, experts. In his diatribe against H. N. Clausen, entitled ***The Church's Response,*** Grundtvig in 1825 coined the phrase "exegetical papacy" (Grundtvig 1906, 420). For Grundtvig this meant that Scripture had been wrongly exalted above both church and confession. Yet the exegetical papacy has only continued to increase since Grundtvig uttered his protest. Just as the pope is the one who has the final word when it comes to the formulation of Christian doctrine in the Roman Catholic church, so one has come to expect, under the domain of historical-critical exegesis, that it is the exegete who can tell us the meaning of the text—and nobody else!

Within the spectrum of theological disciplines, the historical-critical method has led to a sharp separation between exegesis and systematic theology. It is the latter that is believed to have established Christianity's current meaning and relevance and that is therefore seen to stand nearest the church and its proclamation. This separation can be interpreted positively, as when Eduard Schweizer writes:

> Can historical-critical research create faith? Certainly not. Faith is always the gift of God himself. But it can open the way to real listening, to an openness which does not adore a self-made image of God and his word but exposes itself to the living word of God, which threatens all our own ideas and theological constructions, but just so frees us from ourselves to the experience of the living and loving God. That is the point where we have reached the limits of all historico-critical methods. (Schweizer 1982, 11)

However, in the context of university life the situation looks quite different. The Catholic scholar Vogels is considerably more realistic:

> The relationship between exegetes and theologians [the systematic theologian, JG-M] is not always the best. When the exegete finishes his commentary to a text, he usually considers his work completed. He leaves the "theological" reflection to his colleagues. If the student, having followed the analysis of Genesis 3, poses a question concerning inherited sin, the exegete answers that this is not within his field. He sends the student to the systematic theologian. And *he* finds himself in an uncomfortable position. If no exegete is able to master the whole Bible, how can one demand such knowledge and insight of the theologian—where this is still only a presupposition for his own theological reflection? (Vogels 1980, 190f.)

I myself encounter a variant of the viewpoint Vogels describes when a professor of exegesis at Copenhagen modestly describes himself and his field this way: "We are simply shopworkers and craftsmen." One can expand this image and say that according to the self-understanding of historical-critical exegesis, the exegetes are only supposed to put up the house. Who will live in it is not their concern. This modesty is quite equivocal, however. In actuality the matter is turned into a claim by exegetes that if they do not lay the foundations, the whole enterprise of systematic theology floats in the blue air!

The problem with the self-imposed limitations of the historical-critical method is not only a problem at the university. It is evident in the fact that both priests and parishioners run into difficulties when they want to use the results of historical-critical exegesis. For what can a preacher or a pastoral counselor or an ordinary member of the congregation offer against the knowledge that there are so-and-so many sources for Genesis or for the Gospel of John, or that the gospel redactor has had this-or-that intention in the redacting? Both the preacher and the parishioner must necessarily demand that what the Bible says can be actualized and made relevant. Otherwise neither the worship service nor any other churchly activity has any meaning.

The most frequently used solution—which is also evident in the above quotation from Schweizer—is that science (in this case historical-critical exegesis) is one thing, preaching or proclamation (kerygma) another. It is the proclamation, the kerygma, that has to do with the church. But then the question once more becomes this: why is it necessary for a preacher, or for a pastoral counselor, to be able to reconstruct the genesis of a text? Schweizer's claim that the historical-critical method clears the way to an openness that does not worship a self-created image of God is an empty contention. When the exegetes tell us that according to the synoptic Gospels Jesus was crucified on the Sabbath, but according to John's Gospel it was the day before (one of Schweizer's examples, Schweizer 1980, 6ff.), we are made no more "open" for the understanding of the crucifixion—but rather more confused!

Meanwhile, in the present context we must point out that historical-critical exegesis has also had a directly negative significance for the understanding or interpretation of the Jesus-figure, especially because of its synchronic perspective. As is generally known, around the turn of the century it was thought possible to reconstruct "the historical Jesus" and, on the basis of the reconstruction, build a Christian socialism (cf. Schweizer 1982, 14). Historical-critical exegesis, through its various schools and crosscurrents, put to death all dreams of that kind, and Rudolf Bultmann maintained that a "life of Jesus" could not be written. In this regard, he obviously made a virtue of necessity when he used the Pauline word about no longer knowing Christ "according to the flesh" (cf. Glebe-Möller 1987, 98 and notes; cf. also below, chap. 2 n.4). Other exegetes, especially Joachim Jeremias, have tried to reconstruct at least something of what Jesus actually said, and there are certain other indications of a return to the question of the "historical Jesus" (cf. Henry 1979, 125, which refers to books by Jeremias, Bornkamm, Kee, and Keck, and otherwise to Käsemann 1965, 187–214; 1968, 15–47). But still Jesus is seen according to the diachronic perspective as a distant and unapproachable figure whose life and word we perhaps, but then perhaps not, can reconstruct (one of the newest attempts, Meyer 1979, is built on Bernard Lonergan's epistemology), but to whom we can only have historical, not actual, access, in any case.

While it now appears that the cut-'n-paste epoch of biblical scholarship is about to become a past stage (as Vogels also indicates, see above), it is nevertheless the diachronic perspective that is still dominant in exegetical circles. This is the case even with sociological and social-historical study of the Bible, which is becoming increasingly popular everywhere in the world, and especially in the United States, at the present time. Norman Gottwald's monumental work *The Tribes of Yahweh* is a good example. I have no doubt that Gottwald has come further in the understanding of what was at stake in ancient Israel than many of his exegetical colleagues who still play around with the partitions of the Pentateuch.[1] Yet when it comes to the actualities of the understanding of the egalitarian Yahweh that he presents, Gottwald has only the following to say:

> It should by now be evident that efforts to draw "religious inspiration" or "biblical values" from the early Israelite heritage will be romantic and utopian unless resolutely correlated to both the ancient and the contemporary cultural-material and social-organizational foundations. The sole God who liberates an egalitarian people was Israel's cipher for the enduring human project: the wisdom and courage to arrange the variable technological options and social relations available to people within determinate ranges, from stage to stage in social evolution, in such a way that the species as a whole can develop its potentialities. The religious symbolism for such a project will have to grow out of an accurate scientific understanding of the actual material conditions which we face. (Gottwald 1980, 706)

Although I agree in principle with Gottwald, I must nevertheless state that he introduces such a distance between "biblical history" and us that what we can derive from this history, if we can glean anything from it at all, is at best unclear.

And something similar is at work even in recent New Testament studies that have more sociological or social-historical aims, as for example in Gerd Theissen's work (Theissen 1979) or Howard Clark Kee's (Kee 1977). Interest is focused here on the description of the early churches' historical and social conditions, but no lines are drawn forward into our own time—

and the figure of Jesus continues therefore to remain back there, in the distant past.

3. Historical and Systematic

It is not, of course, necessary that a diachronic or historical perspective should result in a distance in relation to the New Testament or to the Jesus of the Gospels. To illustrate this, I shall return for a moment to the separation between "historical" and "systematic" disciplines.

This division is, naturally, not simply an arbitrary expression for an institutional distribution of power. There is—within theology as in other sciences—a difference between going at things historically and going about things systematically when one works with antiquated texts. In classical science-theoretical terminology, one distinguishes between *genesis* and *validity*. If I study Kant's works, for example, I can do so with a view to discovering what presuppositions he started with, what problems in his time and among his contemporaries engaged him, and what influence his solutions exercised. Perhaps I then broaden my investigations to include Kant's own life span, the political and social conditions of the community of which he was a part, and so on. In that case it is the *genesis,* the origination of his philosophy, that I am concerned with, and the perspective of my investigations will necessarily be diachronic.

Distinct from all this is the systematic exploration of Kant's philosophy. Here I would ask whether Kant's philosophical solutions are valid—if it is true, for example, as Kant claimed, that there exist certain "synthetic *a priori* judgments," that is, assertions that we immediately recognize as true but whose truth we cannot prove. That $7 + 5 = 12$, according to Kant, is such a synthetic a priori judgment. I now ask about the validity of Kant's statement. The perspective becomes *synchronic* rather than diachronic. And if, after my own and others' analysis of the problem, I should reach the conviction that Kant was right, I can no longer push his contention away and say that, well, that was the way Kant thought in Königsberg many years ago; I must then also accept and adjust my own scholarship to the presupposition that there exist synthetic a priori judgments. Systematic scholarship, therefore, includes a normative, binding, or obligatory element. The difference between the historical and the systematic approach to texts can thus, in the words of the philosopher of science, Helmut Seiffert, be formulated as follows:

> A *systematic* scientific statement is a statement that will allow something definite to stand as true or false—and here it is only of secondary importance whether the sentence that shall stand as true or false is a statement of propositional significance ("There exist synthetic judgments *a priori*" as over against "There are no synthetic judgments *a priori*") or an authentic normative statement ("Thou shalt not kill" in contrast to "You may as well kill" or "You shall kill").
>
> A *historical* scientific statement is a statement that only registers contradictory synthetic propositions and puts them beside each other without itself deciding for one or the other ("Some philosophers say that there exist synthetic judgments *a priori*, others deny this," or "In many societies it is forbidden to take life, in others it is not"). (Seiffert 1973, 168)

In particularly similar ways we find that there are clear differences between asking what Jesus actually said and did, or investigating the social conditions in Palestine at the beginning of his era, and, on the other hand, discussing whether Jesus' words and works are valid for me or us today. The first type of question is taken up—in the divisions of theological disciplines—by the exegetical (and other historical) disciplines, while the systematic disciplines are engaged with the second type. The fact that one and the same person may do historical scholarship in the study, and go on to deal with the problems of validity in the pulpit, does not rule out this principal difference.

It is important, however, that the historical and systematic approaches to texts can also be combined. That is to say, we work with the texts historically, from the diachronic perspective, but we do it so as to be able to orient ourselves in our own contemporary situation, that is, in a synchronic perspective. We can thus, according to Seiffert, differentiate between two ways of combining the historical and the systematic:

> 1. We can understand a given situation as historically conditioned, and therefore easier to handle.
>
> 2. We can acknowledge, by way of historical consciousness, that a given situation is transitory or partial, and can therefore also distance ourselves from it. (Seiffert 1973, 189)

Transferred to the study of biblical texts, and especially of the figure of Jesus (Seiffert uses other examples), this goes to show that there are ways of talking about Jesus already present in the biblical texts, some of which are bound up with specific historical and social (sociological) presuppositions (for example, "the theological code") and to which we today must take exception. But there are also interpretations of Jesus present in these texts to which we can—and must—still orient ourselves even today.

It is such a combination of historical and systematic perspectives which in my opinion is decisive for the study of theology (as it is in other studies). This—and only this—gives us the opportunity to utilize all our historical knowledge without thereby abandoning the actual, systematic, and normative interpretation of the texts.

4. Two Interpretations of the Gospel of John

Traditional historical-critical exegesis, in its many variations, does not engage in this combination of the historical and the systematic—or better: it does, as we shall see, but it does not acknowledge it! There is, however, a form for exegesis that quite clearly undertakes this combination. To illustrate, I shall include two brief sketches of interpretations of the Gospel of John, one by an American scholar, J. Louis Martyn, and the other by José Miranda of Mexico.

Martyn has raised—with much finesse—the question of why John wrote his Gospel (cf. his two books, Martyn 1968 and Martyn 1978). The answer he gives, briefly stated, is that John's congregation found itself in conflict with the synagogue from which these Christians originally came out (in John's Gospel called "the world"), and also with the Christian Jews that remained in the synagogue (in John's phrase, "who are of this world"). In this situation John formulates a christology that moves on two planes. There is first the (even then) traditional plane, with its transmission of the narratives of the historical Jesus, his death and resurrection. But there is also a second plane in which the same Jesus is described as currently present on the side of the church in its struggle with the synagogue (Martyn 1968, 143ff.). It is this combination of an earlier Christian gospel, which perhaps had interpreted Jesus as the resurrected Elijah (cf. Martyn 1978, chap. 1), and John's solution to the congregation's problems with the synagogue, that together make up the Gospel of John and the christology contained in it (cf. Kysar 1975, 149ff.). This is why it was so important for John to nail down that Jesus is Christ or Messiah (cf. John 17:3). Or in Martyn's words: "Thus, both for John and for his conversation partners in the synagogue, it is *the technical question concerning the messianity of Jesus* that is of extreme importance" (Martyn 1968, 93).

This entire exegetical enterprise does not, however, reach any actual conclusions—except perhaps for the obscure remark that it is only when we start with John's own concepts that his Gospel can speak to our own time ("and initially it is only in his own terms that he can speak to our time," Martyn 1968, xviii). Although Martyn, in his way, has a clear view of the fact that John—that is, the fourth evangelist—must interpret that Gospel concerning Jesus which he has before him in such a way as to relate to the situation in which he finds himself, Martyn stops his investigations at that point, before he comes down to Martyn himself or to our own time.

Not even this historical-critical exegete avoids interpretation, of course, even though in his own eyes, perhaps, he only presents historical facts. For "historical facts" are, as Seiffert says, "the result of an extremely complicated investigation—and interpretation process" (Seiffert 1973, 88). And "even the most elementary manipulation of sources is tied in with an already existing interpretive context" (89). But Martyn, together with the vast majority of his colleagues, most nearly resembles Nietzsche's "antiquarian historian," and shares the limited horizon that Nietzsche describes as follows: "Most things he does not see, and the little he does see he looks at up close and isolated; he cannot measure it, and thus considers everything as equally important, and every detail, therefore, as too important" (Nietzsche 1921, 153).

In José Miranda's interpretation of John's Gospel (Miranda 1977), the tone is altogether different. Miranda belongs among the liberation theologians of our time, and he puts the greatest emphasis on Jesus' command to love of neighbor as a demand for righteousness which is intended for us today, because the "time" of Jesus *has* come in history. But in order to understand our "contemporaneity" with Jesus Christ, it is necessary, Miranda claims, to investigate the Gospel of John with scientific rigor and to utilize the historical-critical method (cf. esp. formulations on p. 73). In actuality, then, we see Miranda proceed the way Kermode describes (cf. below, sec. 7) as being characteristic of professional exegetes: he removes contradictions and determines time and again the correct historical interpretation of the Gospel: namely, his own. Nevertheless, as I have already pointed out, Miranda is not interested in localizing the Gospel or its author in a neutral historical situation, different from his own. It is contemporaneity that is the core concern. John 17:3 is therefore equally valid for us as it was for the original hearers or readers:

> Eternal life consists in knowing the true God—as distinguished from the false gods and mental constructs which we invent to elude God—and in knowing Jesus as Christ, that is, as Messiah. John 17:3 is really the summary of the entire message of John's gospel and of the New Testament. . . . The true God is accessible only in the historical fact called Jesus of Nazareth. . . . The true God reveals himself and consists solely in the imperative of love of neighbor. And love of

> neighbor is no romantic, individualistic sentiment: it means definitive justice for humankind; it means justice and life and heeding every cry of suffering. (Miranda 1977, 195)

To believe that Jesus is Messiah is to be "born of God" and to do the work of neighbor love, for the Word of God is the demand for love of neighbor. To the degree that we seek to avoid this demand, we refuse to believe that the kingdom of God has come with Jesus. But if we believe that Jesus is Messiah, then the lords of this world lose their power (199), then the world is changed to such a degree that even death and physical suffering cease (182ff., in interpretation of John 5:21–30).

I shall not here go further into details of Miranda's dynamic and provocative interpretation of John's Gospel (so provocative that it does not even seem to have been discussed in the exegetes' professional journals!). My point, in the meantime, is only that the utilization of the historical-critical method does not necessarily mean that the biblical texts will remain distanced from readers in our time. Miranda, to a great extent, uses the same scholarly literature as Martyn, but through analysis of it he reaches a much more intense interpretation of John's Gospel—to a degree this is because he holds fast, at the same time, to the systematic interest, the interest in validity.

What, then, is this "already existing interpretational framework" with which Miranda operates? Well, one element in it is his own natural, quite matter-of-course, almost fundamentalistic relationship to the Bible—which is also characteristic of most other South American liberation theologians, while we in Western Europe have developed a much more distant view of the Bible, precisely because we consider it a collection of historical documents in line with many other such sources. Another—just as important—element has to do with his—in broader meaning—political standpoint. Those who, in solidarity with the poor and oppressed in South America, read the Bible, and especially the New Testament, as a message about liberation, will necessarily also read each single biblical narrative differently from those exegetes who hold the political perception that Christianity and politics have nothing to do with each other.

5. The Exegete's Political Attitude

That the exegete's political attitude is actually an essential ingredient in the already existing interpretive context within which he or she works can be illustrated by way of a couple of expositions of the story of the rich man and Lazarus (Luke 16).

In the commentaries a good deal of space is used to point out that the story has *two* points. The one point is that the earthly inequalities are adjusted in the beyond (vv. 19–26), and the other, that one cannot demand a miracle (resurrection from the dead) as confirmation of what God's will is (vv. 27–31). If the commentator or exegete is a little conservative in his or her view of the Bible, it will be affirmed that Jesus himself told the parable to make these two points. So thinks, for example, I. Howard Marshall (Marshall 1978, 634). But more "radical" exegetes, as for example Bultmann, will maintain that the parable, and especially the latter part of it, has nothing to do with Jesus at all (Cf. Bultmann 1968, 178, 196f., 203f.; 1970, 193, 212f., 220). Both wings are in agreement that there may be a number of Egyptian and Jewish models for the story (cf. Marshall 1978, 633), but Bultmann draws from this the following characteristic consequence:

> But such a thought is specifically Jewish, and this version of it can hardly derive from Jesus or the Christian Church; it illustrates the O.T. passage Deut. 30:11–14. But the same is true of the first part, Lk. 16:19–26, which can hardly come from Jesus or the Church, for it breathes the rancorousness of Judaism as it pervades the last chapter of Eth. Enoch, and treats sinners and rich men, the pious and the poor alike. (Bultmann 1970, 220; 1968, 203)

Leaving aside the anti-Semitism that can be spotted in Bultmann's passage—the "mood of resentment" is clearly not characteristic of Judaism (cf. Weber 1970, 247ff.)—the statement expresses something that is typical of Bultmann and his school's separation of Christianity and politics: we must for all the world not put an equation mark between sinner and rich, or between pious and poor! Whenever these equations occur—and occur they undeniably do at many places in the Gospels, if one reads them from a political basis other than Bultmann's—then there must be something involved that is not derived from Jesus or from his church. There must be some form of Jewish (or otherwise foreign) baggage that has been interpolated in the Gospels!

There are other exegetes, such as Jakob Jervell (Jervell 1972, 139–40, 150 n.29 and 31), and Robert J. Karris (Karris 1978, 129–31), who do not share Bultmann's political conservatism and who state that the story of Lazarus is designed to emphasize the continuing significance of the Jewish law, and here especially, the obligation to give alms. But it is Walter Brueggemann's interpretation that represents the most consistent contradiction of Bultmann. In his book *The Prophetic Imagination,* Brueggemann proposes that "real criticism begins in the capacity to grieve because that is the most visceral announcement that things are not right" (Brueggemann 1978, 20). Concerning the rich man and Lazarus, he writes:

> Lazarus is presented as the radical contrast to the rich man. The contrast among other things contrasts the *numbness* of the rich man with the *pain* of Lazarus. . . . The contrast surely operates at many levels. But among other things, the narrative suggests that the rich man who is numbed by his possessions and social status has no future; there is nothing but an end for him. By contrast, the poor man Lazarus, unencumbered either by possessions or by social status, is beset by grief and pain. And, says Jesus, this is the bearer of the future. The contrast, in the context of our discussion, concerns the *numbed one* who knows no future except more of the present, and *the suffering one* who receives newness from the Father. (89f.)

There is no doubt in my my mind that Bultmann, on the one end of the spectrum, consciously depoliticizes the text—and precisely by way of his historical-critical method, which is here clearly used to excise those aspects of the text that are for him most offensive, namely, that it is the poor and suffering that end up in Abraham's embrace. But when Brueggemann, on the other end, politicizes the text in his own way, he is forced to ignore the second half of the story, where it is actually the rich man who is "in grief." And when one and the same text, considered by way of the historical-critical method, can give rise to such contradictory interpretations, it is not surprising that people have recently begun to speculate whether the historical-critical method—even when it is combined with the systematic interest and actualized as it is in liberation theology—is principally flawed as method. From right to left on the political spectrum, and from otherwise widely different scientific viewpoints, we now see a swarm of articles and books on "the demise of the historical-critical method," "the bankruptcy of the Biblical-critical paradigm," and so forth (cf. Vogels 1980, notes). Even among us in Denmark, where historical-critical exegesis has dominated theological education for decades, the protests are now beginning to arise (cf. Nielsen 1981 and 1982).

But what does one then put forth, in place of the traditional exegetes' search for the origins of the text or for the authors' or redactors' "meaning"? Which method should one use in approaching and delving into the text? Roughly speaking, there are at the moment two (related, but nevertheless different) ways that are emphasized. One is the *structuralist* approach, and the other is *literary criticism* (the designation must not be confused with the historical-critical method's textual criticism or study of the literary sources of the Bible). The first approach, which was introduced in Denmark by Geert Hallbäck (Hallbäck 1983)—though Danish linguists and literary critics have been engaged with semiotics and structuralism for a long time—has its origins in France but has been especially cultivated and developed in North America (cf. Patte 1978, and the journal *Semeia*). Likewise, literary criticism today has its foremost representatives on the western side of the Atlantic.

6. Structuralist Exegesis

Characteristic of structuralist (or, in its further development, semiotic) exegesis is that it consciously limits itself to the text at hand, and does not—as in the historical-critical approach—move beyond the text to find underlying facts or the author's or redactor's meaning. The meaning of the text lies within the text itself. The viewpoint, in other words, is synchronic. It can be expressed programmatically as follows:

> The structuralist analysis waives all hypotheses concerned with how the text was composed, how it became a written text; it takes the text as it presents itself for a reading. It considers all its elements as homogeneous facts (*données*), without wanting to distinguish between what is only "redactive" and what could be "original"; it does not compete with the historians in trying to find a supposed narrative that is derived from the first narrators, and which can be discovered among the variations, or on the contrary, which must be ascribed to the commentators of the early church or the evangelists' literary efforts. Instead of separating out the transmitted text, structuralist analysis endeavors to read it in its entirety; and, because it is a question of dealing with a canonical text, structuralists position themselves closely alongside that form in which the text has been transmitted and interpreted through the centuries. (Starobinsky 1971, 64)

It is characteristic, furthermore, that where traditional historical-critical exegesis attempts to get rid of assumed contradictions in the text, there the structuralist-semiotic exegesis considers the contradictions rather as central elements of the text. This appears, for instance, in the utilization of the so-called semiotic quadrangle (cf. Hallbäck 1983, 116f.):

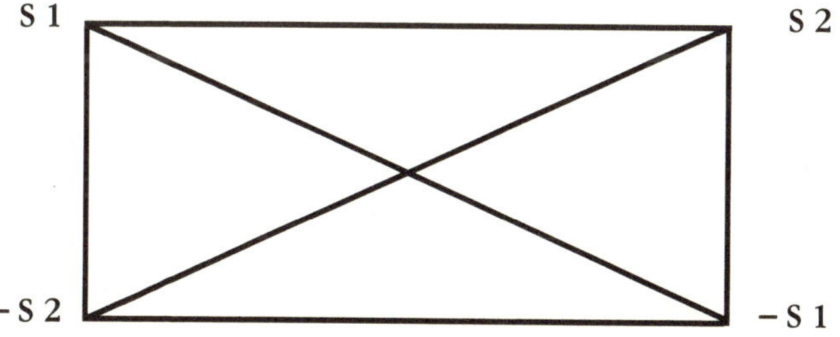

Simply put, the semiotic quadrangle is a theoretical attempt to harness the contradictions in a text, or to show how the interplay between them goes on. In the story of the rich man and Lazarus, for example, we have a "contrary" relationship between being rich (S 1) and being poor (S 2). This develops into a "contradictory" relationship between the rich man and his non-rich status after death (-S 1), and between the poor Lazarus and his blessed state after death (-S 2). This pattern, the semiotic quadrangle, can, according to the structuralists, be found in most texts, and it is therefore altogether false to try to eliminate the contradictions/contrasts in a text, the way we have seen Bultmann try to do it.[2]

7. Literary-Critical Exegesis

Literary criticism, just like the structuralist exegesis, asks very few questions concerning factors and meanings that lie beyond the immediate text. It will focus on the text, and finds—in ways that are less schematic and formalistic than those of the structuralists—certain patterns and lines within the text. An example here is Northrop Frye's discovery of a structure that penetrates the whole Bible: a u-formed pattern, according to which humanity loses the tree of life and the water of life in the beginning of Genesis, and recovers them at the end of Revelations. And within this "large" u-pattern, we can find descent and ascent in various parts of the Bible, even within individual stories (Frye 1982, 169ff.). The story of the rich man and Lazarus can, of course, also be read according to this overall pattern.

Or, we can mention Frank Kermode's reading of the fifth chapter of the Gospel of Mark, where he finds connecting lines and contradictory relationships between the story of the sick young woman in verses 21ff., and the narrative—inserted by the evangelist—of the woman who had menstruation problems, verses 25ff., and further, to the story of the wild Gerasenes in the beginning of the chapter. Here is what Kermode says about the first two narratives:

> This text seems to be continually interested in providing instances of a generalized opposition between clean and unclean,

> and we ought not to dispose of this fact by some historical discourse about Jewish law. The woman, in the present instance, is ritually unclean so long as her hemorrhage continues; but she is at once, by an exercise of power, *dunamis,* relieved of this disability. The girl, dead or supposed dead, is also unclean, or supposed unclean; she is restored by an exercise of power which is, in antithetical contrast, explicit and willed. Between the opposites clean and unclean are inserted—intercalated—figures of sexual or magical force. (Kermode 1979, 133)

And the connection between the narrative of the hemorrhaging woman and the wild Gerasenes is established by Kermode in these words:

> In both [narratives] there is an emission of spirits, clean and unclean. One is followed by an injunction to proclaim, the other by a command to silence. One cure is of an excess of maleness, the other of related effects of femaleness. The lake divides the two like a slash, and the cured demoniac is forbidden to cross it. (135)

As is already clear from these examples, literary criticism does not have much interest in historical facts, as they are ordinarily understood. Kermode, for example, is quite skeptical as to whether such things as "historical facts" exist at all. "What precisely are the facts?" he asks (much as Karl Barth asked Ernst Käsemann: "Tell me, what does 'historical' mean? And 'critical'? And what is the significance of the dash between the two words?" [Vogels 1980, n. 86]). Kermode argues that the Gospels are not historical narratives about factual events; not even the passion narratives are. But when these stories—despite the many internal discrepancies in the details of the four Gospels (for example, as regards the time-frame of Jesus' crucifixion)—nevertheless *sound like* history, or are "history-like," the reason is that they have a "plot." They are told as the fulfillment of a promise that was contained in what the Christians then—or we—call the Old Testament. Such "plotted" narratives do not immediately provide the occasion for raising questions of historicity; rather, they are heard and remembered, and thus appear true.

There is another point, according to Kermode, that shows that the Gospels are not historical descriptions of factual happenings. Mark, for example, utilizes a procedure by which two narratives are woven into each other. We have already observed this process in our discussion of Mark 5. In the final phase of his Gospel (chap. 14), Mark combines Jesus' self-declaration before the high priests (v. 62), on the one hand, with Peter's denial of Jesus (vv. 66ff.), on the other. The two incidents happen together; they point back to Mark 8:32, and are therefore part of the underlying structure of the Gospel: confession and denial, acknowledgment and failure. Mark does not fill in the space between Jesus' self-declaration and Peter's denial. He leaves it to us, to our interpretation, to fill it in: to get denial and confession to fit in with Judas's betrayal and the other disciples' flight—and with the circumstance that the last thing we hear in the Gospel of Mark concerning Peter, the one on whom, according to Matt. 16:18, the church is to be built is, precisely, the denial (Kermode 1979, 115f., 139f.).

And this, then, is the principal part of Kermode's literary-critical viewpoint: the Gospels (and the rest of the New Testament as well) are interpretations (not least of the Old Testament) which invite—and can only live on by way of—further interpretations. Our interpretations, which are necessarily imprinted with our own unique presuppositions ("the already existing context of interpretation"), are not, however, altogether arbitrary. They must follow, partly, the patterns of the text, and partly the rules of interpretation which are given in the institutions of interpretation. Yet the limits and possibilities of interpretation are not determined once and for all. It may very well happen—yes, it could hardly be otherwise—that we in our interpretations can discover facets of a text which the original author could not see. This is exactly the sign of the quality of a text: that it invites more than one interpretation.

The new synchronic perspective that has been introduced by structuralism and literary criticism provides a possibility for a far more varied and nuanced reading of the biblical texts than that presented by historical-critical exegesis. Certainly, this does eliminate the possibility of raising and answering the question of who Jesus was or what he wanted—these kinds of questions can only be posed from the diachronic perspective of the historical-critical exegesis. But by emphasizing the texts' character as—and an invitation to—interpretation, this method is generally in far greater harmony with, first and foremost, the modern view of history, and, second, modern theories of knowledge, than the historical-critical exegesis. For it is not to be used simply to get at indisputable historical facts or at "how it actually was," as they used to say in the last century. As traditional exegetes continue to say: if they give up trying to describe Jesus' life, it is in line with the historical point of view and because the sources are not sufficiently reliable or "objective"—not because it is in principle impossible. But all historical facts are, to refer to Seiffert again, the results of complicated research and interpretation processes. Or to use the philosopher Arthur Danto's expression, all writing of history is "a narrative structure imposed upon events" (Kermode 1979, 117). Moreover, this method includes the possibility that we can read the biblical texts again and again, and so reach a genuine interpretation of them—rather than ending up with a collection of strange and distant "facts" that in their remoteness cannot be binding *on us.*

8. Deficiencies in the Synchronic Method

There are, of course, deficiencies and risks involved in this text-oriented and synchronic method as well. It is remarkable, for example, that an interpreter like Kermode does not allow ethnology any significant role. In his interpretation of Mark 5, as we have seen, he utilizes categories like "clean" and "unclean," "sexual and magical power," but he does not explicate them closely—and there are good reasons why he should. For instance, when the menstruating woman is described as unclean, it has to do with the fact that blood is something that invokes fear in all societies. It reminds people of the ever-present threat of violence, the sign of which is the shedding of blood. People have, of course, always been able to see the difference between menstrual bleeding and violent bloodshed, but sexuality—which is what menstrual bleeding represents—is also related to violence, not only in the form of masochism or whatever else one could mention of sexual perversities, but as a permanent source of unrest and instability in a society or a group (cf. Girard 1980, 55ff.; 1977, 33ff.). Against this background, the story of Jesus healing the woman with extended hemorrhaging also means that he seeks to put an end to violence. As we know from the history of religions, violence can only be checked and counteracted by sacrifice of blood. And it is therefore not unimportant that Jesus' own death was itself interpreted, even in the New Testament, as a sacrifice—or that the Eucharist, at least in the Catholic tradition, is understood as the repetition of this sacrifice. This observation allows us, on the one hand, a possibility of combining Jesus' healing of the woman and his own death on the cross (regardless of whether we today can accept this interpretation or not). And on the other hand, we can here discover some features and interconnections that point in the direction that it is the responsibility of Christians, Jesus' disciples, to defeat violence and bloodshed in the world: "Blessed are the peacemakers, for they shall be called the children of God" (Matt. 5:9)!

Equally serious is the point that an exegesis that moves exclusively on the surface of the text will come to underplay the significance of sociological and social-historical factors both for the text itself and for the interpretation of it. Obviously, a knowledge of the social conditions of Palestine at the opening of our era, or of the sociological structures within the early church, will not in and of itself bring us closer to an understanding of the text. On the other hand, these texts are also answers to the political and social problems of their time. And only to the extent to which these political and social problems correspond to our own problems does the interpretation of the text have relevance for us today and serve as orientation for our own actions. This is the legitimate part of Gottwald's viewpoint, as cited above. If one consistently neglects the role that social or sociological factors play, one will end up with some form of idealistic manipulation of the text, which accepts uncritically what is transmitted, and therewith—in the same way as, for example, Bultmann—one will simply reproduce the political and social status quo.

There are, fortunately, exceptions to this otherwise fairly dominant pattern. One such exception is represented in the Portuguese scholar Fernando Belo's "materialistic reading of the Gospel of Mark" (Belo 1976, 1981).[3]

In the following chapter, I shall attempt to sketch a modern christology on the basis of these viewpoints—though without accepting them in every detail, and especially without trying to reproduce his very complex interpretive apparatus.

Notes

1. See my brief sketch of this work in Glebe-Möller 1987, 102f. Cf. also Niels Peter Lemche's review, Lemche 1982. Characteristically, Lemche distances himself from the book because it allegedly builds on a now-abandoned paradigm in Old Testament scholarship: the theory of the tribal covenant (amphyctiony); he also indicates in a closing note that there are probably not just critical-scientific motivations that lie behind Gottwald's talk of a revolutionary Israel!

2. Hans Jörn Lundager Jensen's article (Lundager Jensen 1980) is a good example of how much the semiotic reading can derive from engaging itself with contrasts/contradictions in a text. As the title of the article indicates, it is especially the "spatial" contrasts that here form the starting point (Lazarus on the street, the rich man at his palace, etc.).

3. In Denmark, Belo's book has been reviewed by Lars Ole Gjesing (Gjesing 1980), and Belo's "apparatus" has been criticized by Geert Hallbäck (Hallbäck 1982).

2. Jesus' Praxis

1. Jesus the Actant

In the semiotic reading of texts there is significant utilization of what is called the "actant-scheme" (cf. Hallbäck 1983, 111). It looks like this:

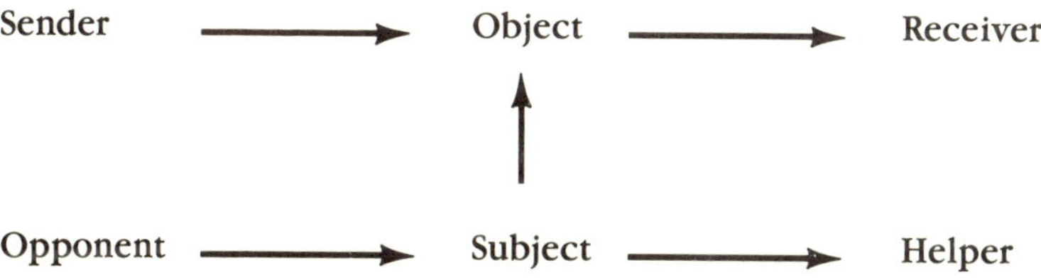

What this means is that in any kind of text—at least texts that are stories, narratives—one can recognize various persons in the text as playing one or more actant-roles. By "actant" one is referring to a person in a story considered not from the perspective of who he/she *is,* but from the perspective of what he/she *does* (Belo 1976, 134 n. 33; 1981, 93 n. 33). Among the actants in the Gospel of Mark, for example, there is of course Jesus himself. The question then is: what does Mark's Jesus do? How can one analyze Jesus' praxis in Mark's Gospel?

According to Belo there are three identifiable levels of praxis in Mark's description of Jesus: that of his *hands,* that of his *feet,* and that of his *eyes* (1976, 177, 330; 1981, 244ff.). Belo derives this triple praxis from Mark 9:43ff.:

> And if your hand causes you to sin, cut it off; it is better for you to enter life maimed than with two hands to go to hell, to the unquenchable fire. And if your foot causes you to sin, cut it off; it is better for you to enter life lame than with two feet to be thrown into hell. And if your eye causes you to sin, pluck it out; it is better for you to enter the kingdom of God with one eye than with two eyes to be thrown into hell.

2. The Hands' Praxis

The praxis that relates to the hands has to do first and foremost with healing. Mark's Gospel speaks constantly about sick people seeking to *touch* Jesus—as for example the woman with the menstruation problem. The story in chapter 5 underscores not less than four times that the woman touched or felt Jesus' clothing. Correspondingly, Mark also describes Jesus as touching or laying hands on the sick—as for example in 7:32ff. and 8:22ff.

It is important to observe this purely physical or bodily aspect of the narratives concerning Jesus' healing activities. In the Lutheran tradition especially, the emphasis is usually so one-sidedly on an intellectually understood forgiveness of sins that how much bodily contact means for the wellbeing of human beings is completely forgotten. As a good Lutheran, I must of course be quite skeptical when I see Catholics in Montreal put their hands on Brother André's coffin in St. Josef's Cathedral in order to obtain a portion of his healing power. But there is more than superstition and magic involved in such touching. There is knowledge of the fact that physical, bodily contact means more than words, or at least must supplement the words. Verbal declarations of love that are not followed up by bodily contact are not worth much! There is nothing strange about the rediscovery—outside the established churches, in neo-religious movements of various kinds—of the importance of touching, laying on of hands, and massage (cf. below, chap. 8, sec. 4).

The hands' praxis, however, refers not only to healings but also, and to a high degree, to Jesus' activities in feeding the hungry.

With his hands he breaks the bread and has it distributed among the masses, say the stories in Mark 6 and 8. The disciples did not understand the significance of the bread—"they were utterly astounded, for they did not understand about the loaves" (6:51b–52)—and even after the second feeding miracle they were still confused as to what it was Jesus did with the bread (8:14ff.). Belo points out, caustically, that "the bourgeois exegesis" still does not understand the meaning of the bread but reinterprets it as a spiritual sign of the coming kingdom of God or as a spiritual reference to the Eucharist (Belo 1976, 205 n. 61; 1981, 149 n. 61). The meaning according to Belo is material: he who feeds the hungry, and in abundance, is the Messiah. Jesus' praxis, when he distributes bread among the hungry, is characteristic of his messianic role. That is why the breaking of bread became a practice among Christians after Jesus' crucifixion (cf. Acts 2 and 4). The words of institution of the Lord's supper (Mark 14:22ff.) say exactly that: when I, the Messiah, have gone away, then my body *is* in that you share bread with each other and with the poor. The Lord's supper, from this perspective, is nothing else than the continuation of his hands' praxis—even though Mark's words "the blood of the new covenant shed for many" (14:24b) already introduces another, more theological interpretation as well (285). I shall return to this theological interpretation, "the theological code," in point 6, below, but I must add here that it is by no means accidental that in what Belo calls "the royal code" (*code basileique*), the gathering at table, around a common meal, plays a central role. We have it first in Mark 2:15, where Jesus and his disciples are at table with "tax collectors and sinners" at Levi's house. And we have it the last time precisely in the story of the institution of the Lord's supper. And in between are narratives such as the first feeding of the multitude, where the command to sit in rows of one hundred or of fifty (the authorized version says, "by companies," 6:40) means that the little circle of disciples is enlarged to include all the world: the feeding of the poor (1976, 332; 1981, 245).

This praxis of the hands—or mutual sharing of bread—has

been given a name in Christian tradition. Says Belo, it is called love (French *charité,* or Greek *agape*). But what about 1 Cor. 13:3, where Paul writes: "If I give away all I have, and if I deliver my body to be burned, but have not love, I gain nothing"? Belo finds a contradiction here (1976, 332 n. 16; 1981, 245 n. 16), but from my point of view, he does so incorrectly.

Read superficially, 1 Cor. 13:3 is of course in clear contradiction with Mark 10:21, where the man we usually call "the rich young ruler" is made to understand that if he wants to follow Jesus and have a treasure in heaven, he will have to give what he owns to the poor. There we find presented a radical demand, one that faces every potential disciple: a complete break with the established order of society. But here, with Paul, it does not seem to be enough to undertake the break and then become a disciple (by distributing all that one has to the poor). Beyond that, love is demanded (1976, 234f.; 1981, 171ff.).

It is clear from the context that the love Paul is talking about can best be described by way of negations (*via negationis*): love does *not* do what human beings in their selfish preoccupations within a power- and class-oriented society otherwise do (or are). That is why love is the greatest of all virtues. The negative description, to my mind, indicates that Paul is most likely referring to a spiritual or even mystical dimension of love—the negative approach, *via negativa,* is also traditionally the way of spiritual or mystical experience. And this spirituality or mysticism, as I shall discuss in more detail in chapter 3, goes far beyond "the hands' praxis," beyond that love that consists of sharing bread with each other and with the poor. One could say that if the Christian praxis *only* consisted of the praxis of the hands—if it *only* consisted of changing economic conditions from a class society to one or another form of communistic society—it would still in the last analysis follow the same economic code as every other praxis we know about. Or in the words of Jesus to the tempter, according to Matt. 4:4 (cf. Deut. 8:3): "Man shall not live by bread alone, but by every word that proceeds from the mouth of God"—where the word of God's mouth, in this context, stands for that which is *not* commensurable with the economic codes of this world.

3. The Feet's Praxis

If the hand's praxis first and foremost shows how the actant Jesus as "subject" helps the sick and the hungry—the "receivers"—we see him in regard to his feet's praxis as the one who contradicts his "opponents" and counteracts their prevailing codes.

The "feet's praxis" is understood generally with reference to Jesus' wanderings throughout Palestine and the further circulation of his message in larger areas. More specifically, and in the first place, the feet's praxis is geographically defined: Jesus wanders first throughout Galilee, then in Judea and up to Jerusalem, and finally the goal is to reach the gentile world. Jesus himself does not reach this goal, but the apostles do. The purpose behind their mission is precisely that the coming of the kingdom of God be announced to the Gentiles. Immediately before Jesus sends out the twelve (Mark 3:13ff.), we read for the first time that non-Jews are among those that follow him ("and a great multitude from Galilee followed; and also from Judea and Jerusalem and Idumea and from beyond the Jordan and from about Tyre and Sidon a great multitude," v. 7ff.). It is this gentile "horizon," evident everywhere in the Gospel, that is behind the sending of the twelve (Belo 1976, 333; 1981, 246).

But when the goal is the Gentiles, this means, in the second place, that all the "codes" that prevailed in the old—Jewish—world are broken down. Instead of being tied together by blood, there are now ties of brotherhood. In Mark 10:29 Jesus says there is no one who has left family or home for his sake who will not receive a hundred times as many brothers and sisters, mothers and children—that is, brotherhood (or sisterhood for that matter) is now the new code. It is remarkable that Jesus does not make any reference to receiving fathers back. In the new covenant, the social and economic authority of the fathers—the patriarchy—does not exist. Mark is here quite in line with Matt. 23:9: "And call no man your father on earth, for you have one Father, who is in heaven" (1976, 236 n. 110; 1981, 174–no. 110).

And it is not only the family structure that is broken down. The entire traditional social structure is obliterated by the feet's praxis. Masters are being exchanged for servants (Mark 10:42ff.), children take precedence to their parents (10:13ff.), and although the man-woman relationship continues in the kingdom, the two are now considered "one flesh" (10:8)—contrary to the prevailing divorce laws that made the husband the ruler and owner of the wife. Belo ends his discussion of this first aspect of the feet's praxis with these words (here and elsewhere, Belo's rather complicated technical language has been simplified a bit, so as to ease understanding):

> The strategy of Jesus leads to the establishment of a discipleship, a *circle* determined by a royal code in which relationships are not measured by those proper to the prevailing social codes, but according to *fraternal service*. Access to this circle is had only by way of a *conversion* that is articulated according to two times: a time of a *break* with the social codes, and a time of *following* Jesus and taking over his practice of service and salvation. (Belo 1976, 334; 1981, 247)

The second aspect of the feet's praxis also contains two points. One is derived from the many narratives that speak of Jesus separating himself from the multitudes. This happened first in Mark 1:35: "And in the morning, a great while before day, he rose and went out to a lonely place, and there he prayed." And it definitively happened at the Lord's supper, which we have discussed above and will return to below.

Jesus' refusal to allow himself to be "closed in" by the crowd means that he rejects the masses' desire to make him their leader in the uprising against the Romans and thus a Messiah after the Zealots' heart. The fact is that if Jesus had accepted such a political "leadership" role, the current and prevailing notions of social hierarchy would have been reintroduced in the kingdom of God. And moreover, his mission would have been limited to Jewish

Palestine. When Jesus therefore separates himself from the crowd —and this is ultimately expressed in the words of institution of the Lord's supper—there is really only one kind of fellowship left in the world: the bread-fellowship. "The absence of Jesus' body is, in the final analysis, a refusal to let that body be established in the political instance, and, consequently, it means liberation from the utopian horizon in the form of a possession of the whole world, but with the exclusion of all domination, even that of Jews over pagans" (Belo 1976, 335; 1981, 248).

The other point in relation to this second aspect of the feet's praxis is that Jesus also withdraws from his opponents. This becomes clear in his avoidance of the cities, "the centers of political power" (1976, 336; 1981, 248). He appears "in secret." When Jesus, after Peter's confession (Mark 8:32), decides to go up to Jerusalem, it is *not* in order to allow himself to be crucified, but in order to undertake a final confrontation with his opponents before turning to the Gentiles. In Belo's words:

> This is movement . . . a progressive extension of the practice of blessing bodies that are freed and satisfying the crowds through the sharing of bread. . . . This *messianic* movement of the narrative . . . *proclaims* the collective Son of man; this political strategy aimed at a worldwide table at which the poor are filled also has a name in the messianic tradition: the name is *hope*. (1976, 336f.; 1981, 249)

4. The Eyes' Praxis

The hands' praxis is love. The feet's praxis is hope. To these is added a third, "the eyes' praxis," which naturally is faith. Jesus is still the "subject." But what does faith consist of? Not of faith in the forgiveness of sins, as a good Lutheran would expect. Faith consists in learning from Jesus to break with the prevailing social codes and "read" his praxis as a salvation of life and body—as feeding of the multitudes, as "blessing"—which ultimately issues in the emergence of the collective Son of man on earth. Three times Jesus tells the sick that they show faith. And each time, it has to do with the fact that despite the crowd—and contrary to Jesus' own family ("and they stood outside")—they seek to come close to Jesus, who then helps them.

The first time in Mark's text is in 2:1ff., which deals with the paralytic man. The next time is in the story about the hemorrhaging woman (5:25ff.) which we have already discussed. And the third time is in the narrative about the blind beggar (10:46ff.). In the two latter instances it becomes clear that the faith that according to Jesus (or the text) has saved these sick persons is precisely their insistence that Jesus can heal them. It is this faith that takes them forward into the physical presence of Jesus—these texts can therefore be read equally well as having to do with the feet's praxis. Even the narrative about the paralytic speaks about such a faith, but there it is the helpers who have the faith.

It appears, in the meantime, that this present narrative also gives an example of the close relationship between faith and forgiveness of sins: "and when Jesus saw their faith, he said to the paralytic, 'My son, your sins are forgiven'" (2:5)—and the rest of the story deals with the question of Jesus' authority to forgive sins. But when a sick person who desires healing, or for whom healing is desired, receives the answer that his sins are forgiven, then sin and sickness are obviously tied together. And that is of course the traditional Jewish (and not only Jewish) way of thinking: illness is an expression of God's judgment, and has its cause in the sick person's sin. When Jesus forgives the paralytic, he lifts the curse that is upon him. This, according to the learned scribes, Jesus has no authority to do—he is a blasphemer. It is at that point Jesus proves his authority by performing, so to speak, the second half of the operation: he heals the man. And the multitude implicitly rejects the scribes' indictment of Jesus for blasphemy. People thank God for the extraordinary things they have seen: that Jesus lifts the curse and makes the paralytic active again:

> And he rose, and immediately took up the pallet and went out before them all; so that they were all amazed and glorified God, saying, "We never saw anything like this!" (2:12)

5. Christology as Ecclesiology

If we read the three forms of praxis—love, hope, faith—together, we have a sketch of Jesus' own praxis as it is narrated and interpreted in Mark's Gospel. Here we have the New Testament foundations for christology. But it is at the same time clear that love, hope, and faith are equal demands upon the disciples. Love, hope, and faith together represent the new code that replaces all the old covenantal codes.[1]

That is how christology becomes *ecclesiology*. And the fact that christology merges into ecclesiology—or Jesus' praxis into the church's praxis—receives its clearest expression in the eucharistic words of institution: "this is my body" and "this is my blood," where the fellowship and brotherhood within the congregation replaces the disciple-relationship to Jesus, which fades away. Jesus does not establish a congregation or a church, as ecclesiastics have wanted to claim, but the church or congregation *is* Jesus, if it is church or congregation at all.

In the discussion of the feet's praxis, above, I have underscored that the patriarchy, as it is known from the ruling social codes in Palestine at the time—and still in Denmark today—is abolished within the fellowship of the congregation. It is important to emphasize this point with relation to the debate over modern feminist theology. What this theology criticizes, and rightly so, is precisely the predominant patriarchal traits in both traditional Christian theology (Christ as man, God as father) and—not least—in the institutional church. The most radical feminist theologians for this reason abandon altogether both Christianity and church and work instead on laying the foundations of a new religion and a new theology, based on the religious experiences of women and bypassing altogether the institution of the church (cf. Daly 1978 and Starhawk 1978; cf. also the list of literature in *Forum for kvindeforskning* 1983). Others, reformist feminist theologians, continue to talk about the church, which they define, for example, this way:

> The church is where the good news of liberation from sexism is preached, where the Spirit is present to empower us to renounce

> patriarchy, where a community committed to the new life of mutuality is gathered together and nurtured, and where the community is spreading this vision and struggle to others. (Ruether 1983, 213)

This definition of the church is in the best possible accord with that reading of the Christian community's praxis which we have found in Mark's Gospel. That the church or the congregation in the course of the centuries has reread or reinterpreted this praxis so as to reintroduce the patriarchy—this is incontestably true. In reality, the church has thereby ceased to be the church or the congregation of Christians in the sense that Mark's Gospel has assigned it. This is also why it appears to me to be an expression of sexism of an opposite kind, and as wrong exegesis, if—as the radical feminist theologians do—one becomes preoccupied with what Jesus *was,* namely a man, and not what he *did:* leave it to his disciples to establish the church as a non-patriarchal fellowship, a brotherhood or sisterhood.

6. The Theological Code

However, the reading of Jesus' praxis or the church's praxis which we have tried to present here, following Belo, is not the only one present in Mark's narratives. Into and beyond the reading of Jesus' praxis as that of the hands, the feet, and the eyes, is introduced and superimposed a second interpretation that I shall here describe as "the theological code" (Belo says simply: *le théologique*). The theological code, just as any other code, is a certain way of reading: a collection of customary and preexisting assumptions out of which a text is read. The theological code is especially recognizable with reference to the interpretation of three features in the Jesus narratives:

A. Although Jesus, according to the narratives in Mark's Gospel, was seeking to avoid his opponents, he was nevertheless betrayed—by Judas—and he suffered death in Jerusalem. This death was necessary—in order that the church's fellowship become a reality, in order for christology to become ecclesiology —but it was not *willed* by the subject Jesus. It was, from this perspective, quite incidental. In other words, it was murder. The theological code reinterprets the necessary/incidental character of Jesus' death by reference to it being *predestined.* This predestination is the kernel of the theological code. By means of it, the *murder* of Jesus becomes his predetermined *death,* "the blood of the new covenant, which is poured out for many" (12:24). And Jesus himself becomes the suffering servant who gives his life "as a ransom for many" (10:45). Read in the light of the actant-model (cf. above), Jesus now becomes the object that alone establishes the "communication-axis": from sender (God) to recipient (the believer).

B. The "Son of man," in the mainstream of Mark's narratives, is a collective and eschatological concept. It stands for the resurrection of ascension of all believing Christians on the final day (Belo 1976, 219, with references to 1 Thess. 4:17). But the theological code individualizes the concept and makes it a designation for Jesus—as for example in the passage just quoted: "For the Son of man also came not to be served but to serve, and to give his life as a ransom for many" (10:45). Here it is Jesus who becomes the exalted and resurrected one, and who from his exaltation is *thought* (imaginatively) to be present in his church.[2]

The Jesus who, to begin with, was the earthly-materially understood *Messiah,* now becomes "Christ"—one can thus say that christology is strictly speaking a product of the theological way of reading. If one accepts the premises of this way of reading the Gospels, what we previously have expressed does not appear to be christology, but (only) "jesuology" (cf. Jörgensen 1983, and my response, Glebe-Möller 1983). But this is quite wrong, as I see it; that is, it is clearly contrary to the reading of the Gospel texts which we today can undertake, with our techniques and on the basis of our interpretive contexts, to accept these premises. I have attempted to say something about the modern interpretation context in *A Political Dogmatic;* in this and the earlier chapter I have attempted to describe the modern techniques. I therefore hold fast with the designation "christology," even though the traditional—and generally speaking predominant—theological code would make a distinction between "jesuology" and "christology" (cf. above, my remarks in the introduction).

C. I have already referred to the reinterpretation that the theological code undertakes in the reading of Jesus' praxis, namely, when the murder of Jesus is made into Jesus' predestined death. A further consequence of this theological reworking is that *salvation* is given a new and different meaning. In the healing narratives—we can once more take the healing of the hemorrhaging woman as our example—salvation means that *the one who is sick becomes well.* In the theological code, on the other hand, salvation loses this present and material meaning and is replaced with a future salvation, realized when the Son of man —now Jesus Christ—returns and saves his elect: when he takes them into his kingdom. But in order for the material and present salvation to become this futuristic salvation, it is plainly necessary that the murder of Jesus be reinterpreted as his predestined death as a ransom for many, or as "the blood of the new covenant shed for many." If Jesus was murdered, and as such against his will, there is no basis for thinking that he shall one day return to save his own. But if his death was predestined, well, then it may well be said that this death has the significance of a future salvation from individual sin and guilt.

In summation, we can say that predestination, christology (in the narrower sense), and soteriology make up the basic elements of the theological reading. But who is it that undertakes this reading? Who is interested in the theological code? Not the community, the fellowship of believers; only "the one and only church," whose leaders are the bishops. As the praxis related to hands, feet, and eyes fails, there is introduced in its place an *ecclesiastical* praxis, where love is transformed into charity, hope is replaced by accommodation to the prevailing social codes, and faith becomes a belief in Jesus' death "for the many."

For Belo, whom I again refer to briefly, it is the theological reading that represents the apostasy from Jesus' praxis or from the first community's praxis (Belo 1976, 377f.), while conversely, according to traditional ecclesiastical-theological reading it is what is usually referred to as "communal theology" that is the cause of apostasy from the original kerygma. Brought to a sharp point, the contrast between Belo's reading and the traditional ecclesiastical or theological reading is a contradiction between praxis and theory (or theology), between Jesus' praxis and the "correct teaching" (orthodoxy) about God. Belo's reading stresses that Jesus' radical break with the ruling social codes is represented by the hands', the feet's, and the eyes' praxis. The theological reading, on the other hand, "ideologizes" the break —makes it an "inner" break—and thereby allows the ruling social codes to stand unchallenged. We thus end up, once again, with our earlier observation that the interpreter's political standpoint has a decisive influence on how a text is read (cf. above, chap. 1, sec. 5).

But is there not an element in the Gospel narratives which transcends all political contradictions? Is the resurrection not just such an element?

7. The Resurrection

It is remarkable that the Gospel of Mark does not contain any resurrection narrative. All exegetes—historical-critical scholars, literary critics like Kermode, or structuralists like Belo—agree that the Gospel of Mark ends with chap. 16, v. 8. This is not the case in the authorized Danish translation of 1948, but even there it is pointed out that verses 9 through 19 are missing from the oldest manuscripts. The most we can say, then, is that we have two texts before us: one that ends with v. 8, and one that ends with v. 19 (plus another one that adds another verse to v. 8). The text that I choose to interpret here—with something close to consensus among the exegetes—is the shorter version.

It describes how three women, after the crucifixion, go out to Jesus' grave at sunrise in order to anoint the body. When they arrive at the grave they see that the gravestone is rolled away, and they go into the grave. There they encounter a young man, dressed in white (who he is, we are not told), and he says to them:

> Do not be amazed; you seek Jesus of Nazareth, who was crucified. He has risen, he is not here; see the place where they laid him. But go, tell his disciples and Peter that he is going before you to Galilee; there you will see him, as he told you. (Mark 16:6–7)

Even though the women hear from the young man that Jesus has risen, and, moreover, receive the direct command to spread this message to others, they do not obey. On the contrary, the narrative ends with these words:

> And they went out and fled from the tomb; for trembling and astonishment had come upon them; and they said nothing to any one, for they were afraid. (16:8)

If one reads the other three Gospels' resurrection narratives (see also 1 Corinthians 15, and the "long" ending to Mark's Gospel), the *reality* of the resurrection is underscored by reference to Jesus' showing himself to his disciples and thus "proving" that he is risen from the dead. Viewed from a literary-critical perspective, the stories concerning the appearances of Jesus do not, of course, constitute proof of a historical fact—if by this one understands what in old-fashioned terms we might refer to as an "objective," "positive" event of one kind or other. The resurrection narratives are "history-like," but they are not examples of historical writing in the traditional sense. But that they are still important within the collected corpus of texts which the earliest Christians produced, cannot be doubted.

From a literary-critical perspective, the uniqueness (onceness) of the resurrection can, of course, well be interpreted as a break with the cyclical pattern of time which was otherwise characteristic of antiquity's understanding of reality (so, e.g., Frye 1982, 72).[3]

This cyclical pattern carried with it a sense of rhythm correspondent with the changing seasons or the rhythm of the day, namely, the concept of a constantly returning death (winter or night). The resurrection can thus be understood as the proclamation that the Son of man has defeated death, especially death on a cross. This, according to the theological code, Jesus had himself predicted: "and he began to teach them that the Son of man must suffer many things, and be rejected by the elders and the chief priests and the scribes, and be killed, and after three days rise again" (Mark 8:31). Again, this reading is also undergirded by numerous references to "the Scriptures"—that is, to the Old Testament (cf. Kermode 1979, 103ff.). The appearance narratives thus confirm the correctness of this reading, as for example in 1 Cor. 15:3ff., where Paul writes: "For I delivered to you as of first importance what I also received, that Christ died for our sins in accordance with the scriptures, that he was buried, that he was raised on the third day in accordance with the scriptures, and that he appeared to Cephas, then to the twelve."

In this interpretation attempt, I have not gone beyond the text itself. And I have not felt pressed to claim that there is a historical experience (or sense-observation) at the basis of the Gospels' resurrection narratives (as I, led astray by Pannenberg, have in Glebe-Möller 1987, 99). The resurrection, and the appearances of the resurrected one, have thus been made explicable and understandable within the framework of the Bible—the Old and the New Testaments—as such.

But the narrative in Mark's Gospel goes against this interpretation, both because it does *not* allow the resurrected one to appear before the disciples, and because Mark's story ends in fear and horror and silence, not in joy and proclamation. In Matthew's last chapter (chap. 28), the women are also fearful, but here the fear they experience is of a different kind—this is clear from the fact that they were immediately ready to obey the command: "So they departed quickly from the tomb with fear and great joy, and ran to tell his disciples" (Matt. 28:8). And the chapter ends with Jesus explicitly giving his disciples the command to baptize and proclaim (28:19f.).

And yet, there are many places in Mark where references are made to a "resurrection," partly Jesus' resurrection and partly the (eschatological) resurrection of all dead. This latter resurrection is linked by Jesus to the question of God's power (Mark 12:24ff.). It is God's power that raises dead bodies. When Jesus makes sick bodies well, therefore, it is the same power that works through his hands' praxis that works in his own resurrection. But this means that faith in Jesus' resurrection is a challenge and a demand for his community's praxis. Will the members of his body touch each other, and through this touching heal each other? Will those who belong to his community share bread and have all in common? In that case—and only in that case—the murdered Jesus has come alive again, raised from the dead in the loving praxis of his community (cf. Belo 1976, 318ff., 388ff.).

This is not to say that we have erased Jesus' resurrection from the story. On the contrary, the resurrection is affirmed, but not as a theological event, a link in the eternally predestined plan of salvation (and still less as a positive historical fact) which only demands faith as an intellectual offering (a faith that is understood as "sacrificium intellectus" or as "fides quia absurdum" is still defined in intellectual categories). It is affirmed as a possibility, as a question that can only be answered in the praxis of love. It is—as it was—up to the readers of Mark's Gospel to give that answer.

By closing his narrative with a reference to the women's fear, horror, and silence, Mark has kept the possibilities open. He poses the question. Mark has not—as the other Gospels and Paul's letters do—given an answer, a fact, that is only to be repeated in the church's proclamation and does not have to lead to praxis, praxis that is unavoidably political. The resurrection, at least as the Gospel of Mark tells about it, does not transcend the political.

8. Deficiencies in Belo's Reading

The *praxis* of the hands, feet, and eyes, the *question* of the resurrection—with expressions such as these, and following Belo, I have sought to lay the groundwork for christology as it evolves into ecclesiology and thus becomes actual, on the basis of the New Testament texts themselves. I do not thereby say that I can follow Belo in all things. I see it as particularly important that the texts do not describe an "actor," Jesus, who from beginning to end performs the same acts, only in two different actant-positions. There is a developmental perspective within Jesus' acts which necessarily falls short in terms of a structuralist, synchronic reading, but which I find supplementary to it and able to make the movement from christology to ecclesiology understandable. When Jesus, as for example in Rom. 8:29, is called the firstborn among many brethren, it means that in the course of his own life—in his own development—he sets forth a possible development also for us (cf. Glebe-Möller 1987, 90f.).

A central section of Mark which expresses precisely this developmental perspective is 8:32ff., where *suffering* is introduced as the way of disciples, the followers of Christ. With his structuralist reading, Belo seems to underplay this text's proclamation of a radical break, a "conversion," even—and especially—for Christians. Where Belo speaks simply of a "change of strategy" (Belo 1976, 119f.), the liberation theologian Jon Sobrino interprets the text with direct reference to what is even today seen to be the way for Christians:

> There has been a change in Jesus' consciousness concerning reality, the future, and the way to inaugurate the kingdom. It is no longer work and active deeds of power that are demanded of him for the kingdom's sake. Now he must display a love fraught with suffering (*v. 31*). His service to the kingdom can no longer follow the old logic, and hence he severely rebukes Peter (*v. 33*). Discipleship no longer means following a messiah in his messianic function. It now means following his own person in all its scandalous concreteness: following him even to the cross (*v. 34*). . . . This shift in perspective is basic for any understanding of Christian morality because it indicates a shift from a line of action based on the universality of certain values (those of the kingdom) to a line of action based on a specific and particular reality (Jesus' own line of action). (Sobrino 1978, 118)

In the last analysis, even the reading of Mark's Gospel which we have presented here is of course also only an interpretation—even though it is one, in my opinion, that we cannot afford to bypass in our future work of interpretation, simply because it keeps so energetically to the text itself. The question, once more (cf. above, chap. 1, sec. 8)—a question not only to Belo, but generally to all exegesis of a literary-critical or structuralist kind—is this: do we not by this reading reduce Jesus Christ to a *literary type* or an *actant* who lives in the text, and only there? Can Christianity exist, or on the whole remain viable, if Jesus was *not* born while Quirinius was governor of Syria (or at another historical point in time), or if he did *not* live a life in history like the rest of us? Does not this form of exegesis result in a new form of docetism (cf. below, chap. 5), clearly contrary to the Bible's own message: the word became flesh and dwelt among us? True, historical-critical exegesis has for several decades given up on the task of describing the historical Jesus, but it has done so for scientific reasons: because it perceived, or believed itself perceiving, that the Gospels were not historical depictions, but testimonies to the Christian community's faith in the resurrected one (cf. Bultmann 1951, 11ff.; 1958, 12f.).[4]

But when literary-critical and structuralist exegesis does not have an interest in Jesus as a historical person, *it is by virtue of its own methods*. It becomes perfectly possible, in fact, to think that he never lived—or that his historical existence was of the same order as Robin Hood's or Holger the Dane's!

This *could* be thought, for our knowledge of Jesus *outside* the New Testament is actually very sparse. We have only a few polemical references in the Jewish Talmud, two passages by the Jewish historian Josephus (which he may not even have written himself), and three brief notes among some Latin writers who all wrote as late as about—or after—the year 100 (cf. Hunter 1973, 11f.).

To this we can answer—and this, in my view, is also the only reasonable and completely satisfactory answer—that even though Jesus may never have lived, we have texts within which he lives, and these texts cannot be removed from our cultural tradition: they are part and parcel of this tradition and contribute to its make-up with hymns, works of art, popular expressions, and much else. Even Nietzsche, a radical thinker in our western tradition who with contempt and scorn discarded Christianity, did not discard the figure of Jesus. He wrote:

> This "happy messenger" died as he had *taught*—not "so as to save men", but to show how one should live. It is the *praxis* he left for humanity: his behavior toward the judges, toward the executioners, toward his accusers and all sorts of slander and scorn—his behavior on the *cross*. He does not turn defensive, does not claim his rights; he takes no step to fend off the inevitable—instead *he invites it*. . . . And he prays, he suffers, he loves *with* them, in those who do evil against him. . . . *Not* to defend oneself, *not* to be angry, *not* to call to account. . . . But not even to go against the evil one—*love* him." (Nietzsche 1921, 251)

This passage from Nietzsche shows another thing as well, namely, that Jesus, regardless of the particular actant-role in which we encounter him, within the Gospels or outside them, is distinguished from most other actants in world literature by placing moral or political claims on his readers. When we read or hear the stories about Jesus, and when we interpret further what we hear or read, then this reading or interpretation demands of us that we take up the cross and follow him—otherwise it is a wrong reading or a mistaken interpretation. It is this state of affairs that still, in our cultural circles, makes Jesus unique and underscores his singularity.

The question of "the historical Jesus," or the question whether Jesus has in fact existed, is of course of secondary importance in comparison with this demand. Only in a theological reading does it become important—and probably because the bishops of the church needed to undergird their authority by referring to their predecessors, the apostles, and their meeting with the resurrected one (cf. Glebe-Möller 1987, 60, and references to Elaine Pagels). And to the degree that the theological reading or the theological code is the code in terms of which Jesus and his praxis most frequently have been interpreted—both in the New Testament itself and in later expositions—to the same degree does it under given circumstances become necessary to discuss the historicity of Jesus and ask the question of the historical Jesus anew. For example, when an existential-theological interpretation such as Bultmann's threatens to completely privatize or interiorize Christianity (cf. Regin Prenter's critique of Bultmann's christology, Prenter 1955, 392ff.). But Jesus' historical existence does not make him unique. His historicity does not validate his singularity.

There is, nevertheless, another sense in which it is necessary to engage oneself with the historical: if the texts are to have validity and Jesus is to be a normative figure even for us, then we are forced to maintain that the texts are themselves answers to historical and social questions, or that they offer solutions to historical and social conflicts. This is a presupposition that enables us in some way to make the answers relevant to our own situation, despite all temporal distance. But if we maintain that the texts are historical in this sense, then the next issue is whether we can relate the questions that they answer—and the conflicts to which they offer solutions—to our own questions and conflicts. This does not appear to me to be difficult. In an era and a society that are saturated with egotism and oppression, both in the national and the global view—and where we are steadily and quietly at work on our own destruction, both politically and ecologically—in such an era and such a society it should be easy enough for those who do not put their head in the sand like ostriches do, to see the parallels to the world in which the New Testament (and the Old) emerged!

9. Does the Bible Belong on the Altar?

At the close of this chapter I want to discuss a viewpoint that has been proposed in the Danish debate concerning the proper understanding of texts. It is the view of my colleague Mogens Müller, who on several occasions has maintained that "the Bible belongs on the altar." In the Danish context, it is of course Grundtvig who is the originator of this way of thinking (cf. above, chap. 1, sec. 2). The polemical point is that the church or worshiping congregation cannot allow itself to be overpowered by the text-expositors, be they academic exegetes or modern fundamentalists, because the church is both logically and historically *before* Scripture. It is the believing community's faith in Jesus that produced the Scriptures, and not the other way around. So the Scriptures belong to the church or the congregation, and insofar as the congregation confesses itself—especially at the Lord's supper—to be the fellowship that Jesus himself instituted, to that extent the Bible must be seen to belong on the altar. Therefore, a correct interpretation of biblical texts, including the figure of Jesus, is possible only within the church's or the Christian community's "space."

All of this would naturally pertain also to someone—like myself—who would claim that the interpretation of the figure of Jesus must lead to political or moral praxis, to a "biblical ethic." The American moral theologian Stanley Hauerwas writes:

> The authority of scripture derives its intelligibility from the existence of a community that knows its life depends on faithful remembering of God's care of his creation through the calling of Israel and the life of Jesus. (Hauerwas 1981, 53)

And again:

> Where such a community does not exist, the most sophisticated scholarly and hermeneutical skills cannot make scripture morally relevant. (54)

Although I am not altogether in agreement with Hauerwas's understanding of the concepts "moral" or "political" (he takes them to mean, as I shall discuss below, chap. 7, the development of moral personality or *character,* "virtuous" people), it is at this point self-evident that one cannot develop normative moral or political prescriptions on the basis of isolated interpretations of the Bible or of Jesus. The "correct" Christian morality or politics can be developed, according to the preceding discussion, only within the bounds of that community that listens to the story of (the narratives concerning) Jesus.

I must, however, raise two objections—that are also, indirectly, exceptions to the claim that Scriptures belong to the church or the Christian community. On the title page of Resen's Danish translation of the Bible, dated 1607, there is a copperplate engraving of a lone Bible-reader (Resen himself, or perhaps Luther? *Köbenhavns Universitets Historie* 1980, 103). The picture is full of symbolism, which I shall not belabor here, but its message is not symbolic. It states, clearly and directly, that an individual who immerses him- or herself in Scripture can find the way to salvation—or in modern terms, to the right moral and political life. It can of course be argued that even the individual Bible-reader reads the Bible only because he or she is a member of a fellowship or a community that ascribes significance to the Bible and its Jesus-figure, that is, that believes in Jesus Christ. But, in actuality there are innumerable instances where the church or the worshiping community does not constitute the immediate context of this Bible-reading or text-interpretation, but where each individual reader interprets Scripture at his own risk, so to speak. It is a consequence of the autonomy that characterizes modern existence, which I have sketched in *A Political Dogmatic* (Glebe-Möller 1987, 33f., 51ff.), and which we may affirm or deplore, but never explain away. The Bible in the hotel room is a visible example. One who spends the night in a hotel room is usually alone, or in any case dissociated from family and church community. Whenever someone reads the Bible in a hotel room, it happens in factual isolation.

My second objection is more essential. It is clear that the Bible —and with it the story of Jesus—is no longer found only in the church's or the Christian congregation's "space." At least since the days of Constantine, we have had the figure of Jesus and the biblical narratives generally disseminated as part of our Western civilization—I have referred to this already. Every Westerner knows of the Good Samaritan! We may have forgotten the story about him, but he has nevertheless come in as part of our system —our legal system, for example. It is on principle against the law in some countries not to come to the aid of those in distress (cf. Glebe-Möller 1980, 83ff.).

If one were to maintain that the Bible and the figure of Jesus can *only be interpreted* within the congregation, that the Bible therefore belongs *solely* on the altar, despite all testimonies to the contrary, the consequence would of course be that Christian morality and politics would become altogether indifferent to the moral and political problems that society generally is up against. The most one can say—and so, Hauerwas does explicitly—is that "our" Christian morality and politics are only indirectly related to social morality and politics: namely, as a "contrast-model" for any and all societies (any and all political systems) that do not know God:

> Unlike them, we know that the story of God is the truthful account of our existence, and thus we can be a community formed on trust rather than distrust. (Hauerwas 1981, 84f.)

But if the contrast-model cannot offer anything more than this, the consequence of the claim that the Bible can be correctly interpreted only within the church's or the Christian community's space will simply be the complete absence of any sense of solidarity with the poor, the suffering, and the oppressed. The consequence is that the church ceases to be the church. The statement that the Bible belongs on the altar makes sense, systematically and normatively, *only* if by "altar" we mean the all-inclusive fellowship of love, hope, and faith. That fellowship not only guarantees the correct interpretation of the biblical texts—it *is* the correct interpretation of the text!

Notes

1. The reference to these three traditional terms may appear somewhat odd in this context, but they do after all have a home in Christian tradition, beginning with Paul. Independent of Belo, Hans Iversen has chosen to use these terms in the context of social analysis and critique (cf. Iversen 1982).

2. This is the reading that Martyn takes account of in his interpretation of John's Gospel (Martyn 1978; cf. above, chap. 1, sec. 4). Belo, working non-diachronically, finds this same meaning also in Mark.

3. On the other hand, it could be said equally well that something dead coming to life again is precisely an event within the framework of the cyclical concept of time (cf. Glebe-Möller 1987, 97).

4. There are important reasons why Bultmann does not have an interest in the life of Jesus. "Hermeneutical" exegesis, of which he is the primary representative, refuses any kind of "objective" investigations of history, in favor of an interpretation that focuses on questions that are posed for our own existence. Engagement with history is therefore "not a neutral orientation relating to objectively identifiable events in the past, but an engagement driven by the question how we ourselves, who stand within the historic dynamic, can come to understand our own existence—i.e., can find clarity as to the possibilities and necessities of our own willing" (Bultmann 1951, 12f.; 1958, 3ff.).

3. Spirituality and Congregational Praxis

1. What is Spirituality?

In the previous chapters, and in *A Political Dogmatic,* I have touched several times on the subject of "spirituality," but without giving anything more than hints as to what that concept contains (cf. Jörgensen 1983, 43). Here I will (finally) attempt to sketch the main features of spirituality. But first a traditional Catholic definition:

> Christian spirituality (or any other spirituality) is distinguished from dogma by the fact that, instead of studying or describing the objects of belief as it were in the abstract, it studies the reactions which these objects arouse in the religious consciousness . . . spirituality studies this consciousness only in its living relationship with these objects . . . it concentrates . . . above all on prayer and on everything connected with prayer in the ascetical and mystical life—in other words, on religious exercises as well as religious experiences. (Bouyer 1963, viiif.)

I call this definition traditional because it presupposes an outdated, namely an intellectualistic, conception of dogmas as unalterable propositions concerning objects of faith which only secondarily—through spiritual exercises, among them prayer—are appropriated concretely. In my own perception, dogmas are an outgrowth of the congregation's praxis, as reflections on what at any given point in time must be considered essential to

Christianity, and they, in turn, lead to renewed or revised praxis. That is why not even the content of dogmas is unalterable. Bernard Lonergan differentiates between the meaning of dogmas and their historicity (Lonergan 1972, 324ff.). The dogmas' *meaning* continues to be true, but their historical context changes. But—as Lonergan himself underscores—the dogmas have *only* meaning within their context. And if, as I have tried to show in *A Political Dogmatic,* the context of the first Christian community was different, in decisive ways, from ours in modernity, then it becomes "meaning-less" to claim that we today are confronted with the same dogmas as the first-century Christians were—for example, the doctrine of incarnation or of Christ's two natures. To say (as Lonergan also does) that the dogmas are permanent in their meaning, because they express truth, cannot be equivalent to saying that our task is simply to accept them intellectually and then translate them into concrete praxis. For then the dogmas would not have meaning "only in their historical context." It is precisely this point that I have attempted to convey by writing that not only does the form of the dogmas change, but their content as well (Glebe-Möller 1987, 6).

But the definition's emphasis on religious experience and prayer (as well as the ascetic and mystical life) does nevertheless point to dimensions which (at least on the surface) go beyond the historical context and, therefore, the political praxis. The first question to be asked, then, is: what can be meant by "religious experience"? The French-Canadian scholar Roland Chagnon gives the following answer:

> The religious experience is in reality one of the strongest and most revolutionary experiences a person can have. . . . The religious experience brings a person into contact with that which he or she feels is the ground of being, the being-abyss. It is therefore not an experience like all others, or an experience which can be brought into continuity with other experiences. The mark of religious experience is a radical break. A break within the flow of time which lets the moment last, and which allows the eternal to be revealed. A break in the monotonous character of space which has a tendency to sanctify (sacralize) the space

> within which the experience appears. A break in one's consciousness of oneself, of the world and of others, which leads forward to new and unspoken horizons. (Chagnon 1979, 23)

With an expression coined by the American psychologist Abraham Maslow, the religious experience is a "peak experience" (24) that may also be classified as an experience of affirmation, of correlation (of the divine and the human), and as ecstatic or mystical experience. These religious "peak experiences" can furthermore be assumed to answer one or more human needs, especially (a) the need to produce or create, (b) the need to love and be loved, (c) the need to understand (31). While those experiences that address the latter need put the accent on "the inner life," it is clear that the answer to the first need must lead to praxis of a political sort. Read on the basis of this scheme, "liberation theology" and other forms of "political theology" are seen to answer the need to create or produce, while most traditional Catholic and Protestant theologies are rather reflections on experiences of love or of understanding.

I have talked about religious experiences and ways to classify them. But do they exist? Is there, for example, such an experience as being in contact with the "being-abyss" or with "being itself"? This appears to me to be incontrovertible. In *A Political Dogmatic,* I have mentioned a few scattered examples. I name, among others, the philosopher Ludwig Wittgenstein as a person who—at least occasionally—could have experiences such as those we have referred to here (Glebe-Möller 1987, 78). Interestingly, Lawrence Kohlberg, in his latest writings, has added a seventh—a religious—stage to his earlier six developmental stages of morality (cf. Kohlberg and Power 1981, 203–59). As examples of persons who have reached this stage, Kohlberg mentions Spinoza and Teilhard de Chardin. In both cases it is a matter of persons who have developed a wholistic, total or inclusive, conception of reality which corresponds to—or is an expression of—the religious experience of being in contact with the depth of being-itself (for other examples, cf. Glebe-Möller 1980, 148ff.). At this point I shall simply enter a reminder concerning

Jacob Böhme, a writer from whose strange works there has emerged much—mostly subterranean—inspiration for innumerable thinkers and ordinary folk in subsequent centuries (my source is primarily Ebbestad Hansen 1978).

Jacob Böhme (1575–1624) saw the sunlight play on a tin pan —and in this apparently banal event experienced the entire content and connection [Danish "sammaenheng," translator's note] of the universe and of history, which he then subsequently described in his many writings, most of which are saturated with biblical and caballistic mysticism. He saw and described the original unity of man and woman—the androgyne Christ—and wrote about Sofia, wisdom, the Jewish mystical symbol for the divine mother.

But the religious experience of being in contact with the ground of the universe was of course not without sociological and biological presuppositions. It is not insignificant, for example, that Jacob Böhme was a shoemaker. Not all shoemakers in the course of time have become visionaries—but there are, among the world's visionary mystics, a strikingly large number of shoemakers (Burke 1978, 38f.)! One can refer, obviously, to the existence of a certain "shoemaker culture" and speak of the tendency of this sedentary vocation to encourage levels of insights which people in other vocations simply do not have the time to develop. Another important circumstance—not least for the understanding of the conflicts in which Böhme landed—is that despite his incontrovertible learning he had never even visited a university. Had he done so, he would most likely have become a priest. The universities of that time were primarily schools from which the state recruited its theologians and pastors. But Böhme, like most of the intellectual nonconformists of his time, had become a learned man outside the university. And this became something on which he—again like many of the other nonconformists of the time—put some emphasis. In a letter concerning his religious experience, Böhme writes: "In my serious searching and desire a gate was opened for me, so that I found more to see and know in a quarter of an hour than if I had attended higher schools for many years." It is important to observe that there seems to be this clear division between the state-educated academicians and those that do not pride themselves on their learning but on their *experience*. This is part of the background for Böhme's conflict with the local parish priest, Gregorius Richter, who scornfully urged him to take a shoe in hand rather than the pen! By appealing to his own religious experience, Böhme ran at cross purposes with the ecclesiastical authorities and put in question their monopoly on interpretations considered acceptable under "the theological code."

2. Feminist Spirituality

In very recent years it is first and foremost the feminist theologians (who of course cannot be considered "theologians" according to the theological code) who have emphasized religious experience and pointed to a combination of sociological and biological factors that serve as its presuppositions. Susannah Herzel, for example, in an essay entitled "The Body Is the Book" (Herzel 1978), writes about woman's concept of time:

> It is the woman's burden and her offering to be more fundamentally connected with time and its detailed process than man. Waiting for something or someone and being aware of the hours as they pass has been a vocational discipline for woman. She is an hourglass in her shape; and she has waited for men, that is, "on behalf of" men and as a complement to their business. Men, however, have undervalued this feminine work, have not acknowledged their need of it, and have certainly not recognized the kind of painful discipline it entails. (106)

And she continues in the same passage with a descriptive correlation of sociological and biological circumstances:

> Women's bodies have taught them the discipline naturally as have their accustomed spheres of work: the garden and the kitchen. You can make neither a flower grow nor a kettle boil more quickly than its given time. It takes nine months for a child to come. A woman can only wait. And each month in her life there is a heaviness, dragging her down to a slower pace and

> into a "low key." But the waiting is not necessarily an inactive period. In their representations of women waiting, artists have instinctively depicted them as sewing, weaving. In the realm of language and thought such a time for connecting and reflecting is as important as the time of sowing and disseminating. In such a process, the new grows out of the old, rather than replacing it. (106)

Herzel's reflections are interesting in several ways. They point to the fact that because of social as well as biological reasons women have deeper rootage in the life-world, and are therefore, among other things, more removed from modernity's abstract, linear concept of time (cf. Glebe-Möller 1987, 78). They also indicate that traditional female activities such as sewing or weaving—in the same way as the artisanship of shoemakers—throughout the centuries have formed good soil for religious experiences. But above all, they stress that *experiences* are more important than all abstract logical-theological distinctions. It is by putting emphasis on such matters, which are common to all feminist theologians, that the feminists—just like Jacob Böhme in his time—tend to fall out of line with the theological authorities. Sheila D. Collins writes:

> Because the theology of the feminists refuses to adhere to authoritative methods, traditional theologians may be tempted to label it "untheological" or "unscholarly" and therefore dismiss its content. When this occurs, feminists are likely to respond the way Mary Daly did to a critic at Yale Divinity School who objected that her lecture was not "theology." "I couldn't have cared less whether what I was doing was or was not theology in his terms," she has stated. "As far as I am concerned, I was involved in a search for God. The label does not matter." (Collins 1975, 42–43)

The cosmic experience, the feeling of being in contact with the ground of being, also emerges in the feminists' perspective again and again (cf. Sjörup 1983, also Glebe-Möller 1987, 78). No one among feminist writers has described this with any greater strength than Margaret Atwood, in her novel *Surfacing* (cf. Christ 1980, chap. 4):

> It is the story of a young woman who together with three compatriots returns to an area of the Canadian wilderness, where she grew up as a child, in order to search for her father, who has disappeared. While the other members of the party are typical representatives of modern civilization, the heroine experiences more and more of an identification with untouched nature and the forces at work in it. At the end of the story she leaves her friends in order to be alone in the sacredness of nature. She discards her clothes, crawls on all four, lives on roots and wild berries—her humanity returned to nature:
>
> "The animals have no use of speech,
> why speak when you are a word
> I lean up against a tree, I am a leaning tree
> I break out in the clear sun and bend
>   together with my head to the earth
> I am not an animal or a tree, I am that
>   which trees and animals move and grow in,
> I am a place."

It is easy to understand why feminist spirituality must acquire a *wholistic,* all-inclusive character (cf. Collins 1975, chap. 5, entitled, "The Personal Is Political: Towards a Wholistic Ethic"). It is characteristic that even *the body* is drawn in, for the body belongs within our relationships to each other and to the natural environment. Sheila D. Collins, for instance, writes about the false contradiction between person and body—something that is foreign to all female experience, especially during pregnancy—and about the necessity of once again coming into contact with our bodies and "learning their special rhythm and message." And she continues:

> Body knowledge is also our window on the world. Through an understanding of and participation in the ecology of the body we can gain a better understanding of the ecology of the natural world and our place in it. The premonotheistic peoples understood this relationship better than we do, as do American Indians—at least those who have not been corrupted by the white man's culture. We have come to a point in the history of civilization where, if we do not begin to understand these relationships, we may very well end by destroying everything. (Collins 1975, 182)

Herzel, whom we referred to earlier, also emphasizes the bodily dimension of spirituality ("the body is the book"). She has written a historical study of the World Council of Churches' division of "Women in Church and Society," and here she closes with some reflections on women's unique prophetic ability of "seeing in." As will be clear from my references to Jacob Böhme and others, I cannot consider this ability something especially feminine. But it is also feminine, at any rate, and perhaps women have some privileged access to it in and with the biological and sociological circumstances mentioned above. Herzel, in any case—and, on the whole, contrary to many of her sisters—thinks that this is what makes it possible to consider the figure of Mary positively:

> It is inside her body that the Divine is born. It is her inwardness which is the sign of her ministry. Her body is the vessel inside which the reconciliation of the two great polar opposites—God and man, heaven and earth—is born. She is—in the spaces of her womb and her heart *and her mind* (she said Yes; she was not in a trance!)—the God-bearer (Theotokaos), the carrier of wholeness. In this respect, she did nothing outwardly startling. Rather, she accomplished something inwardly, secretly, silently. By her active *response,* she bore that primary cross or conflict represented by the polarity of God and man. (Herzel 1981, 154f.)

Susannah Herzel is able, as a feminist theologian and out of the experiences of women, to interpret the doctrine of incarnation in a new way—and definitely not in harmony with the theological code. It is not Jesus' preordained birth and atoning death for our sins that are in focus here. Viewed from the perspective of spirituality, it is that otherwise fundamental conflict—between being at one with the cosmos and the divine or only belonging to earth (and the human world)—that Mary overcomes, in her body and her consciousness. And this leads naturally to the question whether we can find something of this spirituality, what I have tried to circle with the help of feminist theologians today, in the New Testament Gospels.

3. Spirituality in the Gospels

An essential aspect of spirituality is the incorporation of the body and of bodily connections with the natural environment. This aspect is quite unessential to the theological code, intellectualistic as it is. But the hands' praxis—the praxis of healing and the fellowship of shared bread—is very definitely related to the body and has to do with the incorporation in nature.

When Jesus *touches* the sick and teaches his disciples—his congregation—to feed the hungry, it is far more than deeds of charity that spring from sympathy with the sick and the suffering (or whatever else, with more or less sentimentality, one can find to say about it). It is an expression of a spirituality that knows that only somebody with a touched, healthy, and fed body can fully enter into connection with the ground of being and existence. Every form of bodily deprivation means *in reality* a lack of the possibility of achieving full contact with the natural world around us. The blind cannot *see*—not colors, light, sun, moon and stars, plants, animals, and other human beings. The paralytic cannot *walk*—cannot feel the earth underfoot, or move in the rhythms of dance, or experience the wanderer's fellowship with both people and wildlife. And the hungry feels only hunger and is unable to participate in the larger joys and sorrows of existence or human life. By touching and healing and feeding those in need, Jesus puts them in contact with that cosmic *togetherness* (or solidarity) that the feminists talk about.

It does not make sense—according to my arguments in chapters 1 and 2—to ask whether Jesus himself felt in touch with the essence and ground of existence. We have looked at Jesus-the-*actant,* at what Jesus does, and have principally declined to speculate about his own experience. But there is no doubt that the New Testament texts do work with the motifs of spirituality. This is particularly the case in John's Gospel. In the so-called high-priestly prayer (John 17), Jesus prays to the Father,

> Holy Father, keep them in thy name, which thou hast given me, that they may be one, even as we are one. (17:11)

And a little later in the text, Jesus prays,

> that they may all be one; even as thou, Father, art in me, and I in thee, that they also may be in us, so that the world may believe that thou hast sent me. (17:21)

These words, which form the motto of the ecumenical movement, say only superficially that the separated churches must be reunited in order that their missionary task can be successful. Read in context, it is not of course the need for cooperative fellowship among separated churches or denominations that is dealt with here, but just the Christian community, the communion of Jesus' disciples. To the degree that this fellowship exists, Jesus is also one with the Father, in touch with the ground of existence—and so is the church, on its side. And "the world," when it sees the fellowship of this communion, and its praxis of love, can then also see that here is created real contact with the depth of being.

And we can point to the role that prayer plays in the Gospel narratives. Prayer, as we have already said (cf. above, quotation at the beginning of sec. 1), is one of the manifestations of spirituality. It is, briefly stated, the expression of a willingness to yield—beyond all rationality, whether instrumental or communicative—to "the power to be in everything that exists" (Lögstrup 1978, 225f.). It is set forth, paradigmatically, in the prayer Jesus taught his disciples: "Our Father, who art in heaven." Or in the prayer Jesus himself prayed in the garden of Gethsemane, when his "strategy (or praxis?) of the feet" had broken down and the only thing he could say is, "Abba, Father, all things are possible to thee; remove this cup from me; yet not what I will, but what thou wilt" (Mark 14:36).

I can illustrate this conception of prayer by the following reflections of Rosemary Haughton, a well-known American author of books on spirituality. She writes:

> The word "prayer" is, to many, a narrow and specialized word. To pray is to do something extra. It is good, perhaps even the highest good, but quite apart from actual *doing*. Indeed we can

> manage very well without prayer and most people do. But without prayer what is it that we do? Prayer is not a separate activity, but simply a living from the centre. . . . It is the place to which the psalmist turns, finally, driven by his desperate need to understand the congruence of misery and prosperity, of the guilt of the oppressed and the "untroubled" minds of the oppressors, the "punishment" of the innocent and the "sound and sleek" bodies of the proud [cf. Psalm 73]. When he was "stupid and did not understand" it was because he was still under the sway of the phantom world of false autonomy, but *all the time* the reality was there, it needed only the courage of love to discover it:
>
> Yet I was always in your presence,
> You were holding me by my right hand.
> You will guide me by your counsel
>   and so you will lead me to glory.
> What else have I in heaven but you?
> Apart from you I want nothing on earth.
> My body and my heart faint for joy;
> God is my possession for ever.
>
> In this place, and here alone, Wisdom is at home. (Haughton 1981, 312)

As is clear from this passage (where Haughton quotes Ps. 73:23–26), prayer is an expression of the fact that a person's need to understand cannot be satisfied on the normal intellectual plane. Here, religious experience steps in, expressed in the words of prayer. It is a movement out of the center, it grasps reality itself, and it corresponds to the need to understand, not the need to do something. It does not represent praxis—or at least, only secondarily so.

But it is precisely this that makes spirituality dangerous, in my view. Spirituality is an expression of religious experience; it is there, and is perhaps stronger than all other experiences—but it operates, always, on the edge of pure passivity, and therefore on the edge of the world as it actually is.

This is not so in the New Testament, as I see it. Jesus' prayer at Gethsemane does not express acceptance of the coexistence of misery and riches. Even though Jesus' strategy has failed, the contradiction between misery and riches remains in force. Spirituality is the basis for the praxis of love, but the praxis of love consists precisely in this: to fight against riches, oppressors, and "the proud." This is what it means when Christians are said to be called to live "according to the Spirit" (spiritus-spirituality, cf. below, sec. 6). Outside the New Testament, however, spirituality is often in a very ambiguous relationship to praxis—or to what is of course the same, politics. This is especially so when it concentrates on "the inner life." I shall exemplify this ambiguity by way of a number of examples.

4. Spirituality and Praxis

In the Western world it is especially the Unitarians, with their dogma-free form of Christianity, who nurture a special sympathy for spirituality. It is more than circumstantial that many of the American feminists and feminist theologians have their books published by the traditional Unitarian publishers, Beacon Press in Boston. One need not wonder, when in the Unitarian hymnal one encounters a hymn like this, by Monroe Beardsley:

> From all the fret and fever of the day,
> Let there be moments when we turn away,
> And, deaf to all confusing outer din,
> Intently listen for the voice within.
>
> In quietness and solitude we find,
> The soundless wisdom of the deeper mind;
> With clear harmonious purpose let us then
> Bring richer meaning to the world again.
> (*New Hymnbook,* n.d., #84)

What is described here is the wisdom of that deeper consciousness which we are able to find within ourselves, and only when we listen to the inner voice. But what does this wisdom mean—the wisdom that the devotees of spirituality so often talk about? Beardsley gives one indication: it brings a richer meaning to the world. In other words, wisdom satisfies the need to understand, but what kind of actions it will result in, even in the best of cases, is unclear.

I shall include another example of spirituality, one that also derives from the need to understand, in this case suffering, and that answers by reference to an experience of correlation, namely, an identification with the crucified one. The Indian priest Subir Biswas was in the hospital six weeks, and could not in all that time move or change his position. But he was still able to reflect religiously on his experience. He writes:

> Lord, when you were crucified, you too could not move. My suffering was so insignificant and yet I was so weak and so often depressed. On the cross you prayed for others but I found it so hard to lift up my heart. Thank you, Lord, for giving me this time. You forced me to remember the thousands of your children in this city [Calcutta, JG-M] who lie for years and years in cancer and TB hospitals without any hope of recovery. I thank you for reminding me of old people who will never move out of their rooms again. It is so easy to grow callous, Lord; it is so easy to visit them and feel virtuous. But you are good, Lord; you give us a little taste so that we can love and feel again. Help us to always remember and teach us again if we forget. (Poulton 1982, 59)

In this experience the impulse to *do* the work of love is naturally present. And Subir Biswas did not spare himself in this respect. But the identification with the crucified one does not, strictly speaking, have to lead to actual praxis. Often a religious experience that corresponds to the need to love and be loved, to *love itself,* may in actual fact prove to have an inner relationship to political conservatism.

The experience of love is perhaps *the* single experience that one most often focuses on in spirituality. In love, humans transcend themselves. The love of God, says Bernard Lonergan, is "the fundamental fulfillment of our conscious intentionality" (Lonergan 1972, 105). Paul expresses the same theme in 1 Corinthians 13 (cf. above, chap. 2, sec. 2). In the next chapter we shall look at a modern exposition of that passage. The experience of love—of loving or being loved—can be said to transcend our ordinary experiences, with each other and in our normal social existence. To a degree, there is in this experience some "kernel of resistance" in relation to the oppression that the system constantly lays over our life-world (cf. Glebe-Möller 1987, 54). So, when Jürgen Habermas, in an interview in 1977, said that the legacy of religion, the humanizing power of the religious traditions, cannot be brought into modernity *as religion,* his viewpoint is obviously too narrow (cf. Glebe-Möller 1983b, 182).

The religions of the world are *not simply* a series of successively developed hermeneutical systems, where Christianity and the other higher religions represent a last, now past, stage. Religions are also—and this goes for Christianity as well as the other higher religions—spirituality. But this "ground of existence," this transcendence with which a human being comes into contact through the experience of love—which is also symbolized in the theological code's image of Jesus dying for our sake—does not in and of itself lead to political praxis, to fellowship, to the cancellation of oppression. This is clear from an analysis of the charismatic movement within Roman Catholicism, as presented in a study from Quebec, the French-speaking part of Canada. Here, large charismatic rallies held in the late seventies could gather up to thirty thousand people. Typically, the basic structure of the movement has come to expression in the prayer groups. In the prayer fellowship within these groups the participants have an experience of loving God and each other—and of being loved, by God and by each other. Here as elsewhere in the charismatic movement the religious experiences also come to expression in a "baptism of the spirit" (following laying on of hands) and glossolalia, speaking in tongues. It is all pure spirituality. Moreover, if we study more closely the social and political circumstances out of which the charismatics come, it is clear that by far the largest number are recruited from the lower range of the middle class, are between fifty and sixty years of age, and are on the whole supporters of the status quo in economic and political matters. This is how Roland Chagnon describes the charismatic movement ("the charismatic renewal") in Quebec:

> By its insistence on an intensely religious experience, on the inner conversion to Christ, on the immediate fellowship which is established in negation of all personal and collective conflicts, the charismatic renewal helps people endure and tolerate the ills of society, and thus creates a convenient and non-threatening run-off from actual social evil. Seen from the viewpoint of social change, its effects can only be demobilizing. The a-political attitude within the charismatic movement can in fact be translated into a precise political standpoint: to serve as warranty for the existing liberalistic society. (Chagnon 1979, 111)

It is observations and analyses such as these that cause a socially engaged Canadian Catholic theologian like Gregory Baum to pronounce that we cannot turn back to "an earlier spirituality" that often made Christians indifferent to social questions and allowed them to "live joyously and peacefully face to face with serious social evils and oppressive institutions." In other words, the spirituality of the past—and that it is still not altogether passé is evidenced in the charismatic movement!—was not able to create a core of opposition to systematic oppression, much less a contradiction to the fundamental inequity and injustice of the liberalistic-capitalistic (or, for that matter, socialistic) society. But Gregory Baum nevertheless maintains that there is also another, newer form of spirituality which does not have such reactionary, society-stabilizing consequences, but which on the contrary leads to social and political praxis. He writes:

> I wish to argue that the church's new social teaching [the Roman Catholic, JG-M] is based on, and accompanied by new religious experiences, at odds with pietism, which explode the walls of self, reveal to people that they are embedded in classes or movements and generate a new sense of solidarity with others. This transcendence of soul-centeredness is also experienced as divinely grounded; as a gift, as something to be grateful for, as God's presence. The only way a person lives authentically is to let "the others" become part of his or her own self-destination. (Baum 1981, 46f.)

And he continues, now with positive reference to classical spirituality:

> Catholic activists do not see any conflict between political radicalism and the mystical tradition. The ancient Catholic teaching of the *via negativa,* the dialectical negation of all God-language has a special affinity to new spiritual direction of the contemporary social gospel. (47)

Baum does not himself follow up with the details of his argumentation, but we can at least indicate how it might go. *Via negativa* (or *via negationis*)—the negative way (or the way of negations)—is often dealt with in the philosophy of religion as an epistemological-theoretical-theological problem: how does one obtain knowledge of God, of divine being and divine properties (cf., e.g., Holm 1955, 202f.)? The epistemological problem is approached by way of negation: only by renouncing all positive properties in God can God be adequately described; only by claiming not to know God, does one know God. With Augustine's expression, *melius scitur Deus nesciendo* ("God is best known when one does not know him," quoted from Casserley 1961, 40). It is especially within Catholic medieval mysticism that the via negativa was nurtured, as can be seen for example in the old English tractate, *The Cloud of Unknowing* (in Danish translation by Haahr and Pedersen 1983).

For the anonymous author of *The Cloud* there are principally two ways to live the Christian life: either as an active life (*via activa*) or as a contemplative life (*via contemplativa*). The biblical models of these two ways of life—to which the author makes repeated references—are Martha and Mary, respectively. Martha busily performed works of love. Mary Magdalene meditated. But meditation is itself its own purpose, or rather, its purpose is the communion with God in love. Everything else is secondary or indifferent by comparison. "One thing is needful. Mary has chosen the good portion, which shall not be taken away from her" (Luke 10:42). The book then describes how a person, through constant spiritual exercises, can ascend toward the cloud of unknowing and there, in the midst of ignorance, know God. "Ignorance" means that one cannot approach God through reason or knowing. But neither can one approach God —or God the believer—through the senses or feelings. On the contrary, one must be detached from all thoughts of self or of other creatures in order that the soul may be one with God. The author does not have very high thoughts about the body either; for him, everything must be understood as—and be—spiritual. And yet, he makes clear at the same time that the via negativa is also a *way,* in the sense in which Christianity, ever since the days of the early church, has been called "the way": namely, as a distinct way to live and act. For when one's purpose becomes to reach upward to the cloud of unknowing, one has at the same time said that all the things that normally mean something on earth, money and power (the two primary forms of "the system," cf. Glebe-Möller 1987, 54), must be negated. The anonymous author does not say this in so many words, but it is the logical consequence of his thinking. And that is how spirituality can be known to lead to a distinctly critical standpoint in relation to present existence.

5. Creative Spirituality

Within Christianity, the concept of spirituality has been retained primarily in the Catholic tradition. Among Protestants, ever since the Reformation, there has been an overtone of self-righteousness associated with the term. According to traditional Reformation thought, those who exercised the spiritual disciplines—especially monks—were seen to have distorted the good news of salvation-by-faith-alone and replaced faith with good works. That is one reason, among others, that the monasteries were torn down and the monastic orders were disestablished wherever Lutheran or Reformed Protestantism came to be the official religion. With this, naturally, the "subversive" side of spirituality was also pushed into the background and replaced with the ideal of a socially supportive life in one's own given calling and estate (cf. Glebe-Möller 1987, 64f.).

But it is precisely this "subversive" or critical side of spirituality which in recent years has been emphasized within a long list of works by Catholic theologians (Baum's "new spiritual direction"). As an example, we can mention a book by an American,

John Francis Kavanaugh, *Following Christ in a Consumer Society* (Kavanaugh 1981). Over against the consumer society and its "commodity form" (described in Marxist categories, although Kavanaugh is not a Marxist!), Kavanaugh puts in place "the personal form." He contrasts, for example, the "thing-realities" and the "person-realities" in life by way of the following scheme:

Thing-Reality	*Person-Reality*
Having	Being
What is	What we can be
Human Skepticism	Faith and fidelity
Human paralysis and doubt	Hope and trust
Individual isolation	Love
Unfreedom as final condition	Freedom as final condition
Death	Life

(Kavanaugh 1981, 97)

It is Kavanaugh's contention that "lived Christianity"—Christianity in the personal form—can withstand the commodity culture. He points especially to the traditional elements of resistance in the Catholic spiritual tradition: community, prayer, the seven sacraments, the ordered life (116ff., 119ff., 123ff., 135ff.). But the aim is not "a strengthening of the inner life" in isolation from the social context. On the contrary, faith and social justice belong together:

> Only when faith and justice are seen as being mutually constitutive, only then is the social and cultural content of spirituality acknowledged and acted upon, only then does the sanctification of human life take place and the saint emerge. (Kavanaugh 1981, 156)

Prayer—not least the Lord's Prayer, the paradigm for the Christian's spirituality—receives a correspondingly creative meaning in this new movement. Leonardo Boff calls it "the prayer for perfect liberation." For example, when he exegetes the second stanza of the Lord's Prayer—"hallowed be thy name"—he says:

> We are not sanctifying the name of God when we erect church buildings, when we elaborate mystical treatises, or when we guarantee his official presence in society by means of religious symbols. . . . We sanctify the name of God when by our own life, by our own actions of solidarity, we help to build more pacific and more just human relationships, cutting off access to violence and one person's exploitation of another. God is always offended when violence is done to a human being, made in his image and likeness. And God is always sanctified when human dignity is restored to the dispossessed and the victims of violence. (Boff 1983, 49; cf. Crosby 1977)

This active form for spirituality is characteristic of South American Catholic liberation theology—of which Boff, of course, is a leading representative. If we put it in relation to the fundamental needs listed in section 1, we find clear evidence, as already mentioned, of the need to produce. But it is not only South American theologians that speak and write about—and out of—such an active, creative spirituality. Third world theologians do the same, over a broad front. The Taiwanese Choan-Seng Song, who is Lutheran, says explicitly that creativity and spirituality belong together:

> A truly creative spirituality is one that enables us to realize and experience the divine presence in all that we do, not only in religious worship, but also in all realms of our activities. It breaks down the barrier between the sacred and the profane, the religious and the non-religious, the holy and the secular. To encounter other human beings in the rough and tumble of this world, to experience life in the midst of death, and to perceive meaning in the face of meaninglessness—this is spirituality. (Song 1979,3)

When the main character in Margaret Atwood's novel, which I referred to earlier, at long last decides to return to the city ("civilization") with her new-found or rediscovered self, her new message was this: "this above all: refuse being a sacrifice . . . give up the old belief that you are powerless"—and with this she joins the many other feminists who speak out of the same active and creative spirituality (cf. Song, who explicitly includes the feminist movement among the new manifestations of spirituality, Song 1979, 2f.).

The various forms of spirituality belong together, just as the need to love or be loved belongs together with the need to understand and the need to produce or act. But as we have seen, a meeting with the depth of being, or however else one prefers to express it, can have—has in fact had—a wide variety of political consequences. No form of spirituality is above and beyond the political. Spirituality manifests itself—if it becomes manifest at all—*in this world,* and this world is manifestly political, whether one accepts it or not. Spirituality can ignore the political world, for example, by going behind its back to something "pre-cultural"—this, as it appears to me, is the tendency in the Lögstrup form for spirituality that I mentioned above (sec. 3)—or to a pure correlational experience, as in the case of the charismatics.

But even these forms of spirituality are political. By not seriously placing a question mark on the existing political system, they only affirm and confirm it. Or spirituality—as in the latest examples I have mentioned here—can be political simply by pointing to or underlining other forms of life than that of the system. This is not to say that spirituality can be *identified* with "the political." Religious experiences can only unfold in contexts that are political. But the experiences are not identical with the context. This is the correct core in the argument of those theologians who will not acknowledge that the cause of peace is the cause of Christians, the cause of the church. But it does not follow that it is not a part of churchly praxis to work for peace in social and political contexts.

6. Spirituality Must Be Practiced

Spirituality, where it exists, is evoked by and founded on fundamentally religious experiences. It involves a break with previous ways of living and thinking—what in traditional Christian terminology is called "conversion." This break or conversion means that the Christian no longer walks "according to the flesh, but according to the spirit," as it is described in Rom. 8:4–12 and Gal. 3:3–6. "The spirit," in the Christian tradition, is called "the Holy Spirit" (*spiritus sanctus*), and spirituality is then, according to this terminology (which in my opinion we will have difficulty passing on into modernity, cf. Glebe-Möller 1987, 106) the "fruit of the Spirit" (a spirituality of the Spirit, *spiritus-spirituality*). But it is not only in Christianity that spirituality is known. Spirituality is naturally present in all the higher religions. Gandhi, for example, in his strategy of nonviolence, combined elements from both Christian and Hindu spirituality (cf. Song 1979, 28ff.). And even though spirituality involves breaks and conversions, it can and must also be learned and practiced—which again requires certain techniques and exercises as is indicated in the quotation at the opening of this chapter. All the great masters of spirituality have pointed to ways in which one may "train oneself" in walking after the spirit. I have mentioned the anonymous author of *The Cloud of Unknowing*. One of the most famous named examples is the founder of the Jesuit order, Ignatius Loyola.

It is not just happenstance—though still for a Western Protestant somewhat surprising—when Jon Sobrino closes his book on *Christology at the Crossroads,* cited above, with an exposition of the image of Christ in Ignatius's *Exercitia spiritualia* (cf. Sobrino 1978, 396–424). According to Sobrino, the spirituality one can learn with Loyola as one's guide is not a passive but an active spirituality. The "exercises" related to godly love shall not lead to contemplative observation of love but to active practice of love:

> You see that God's presence in his creation is never at rest; it is constantly active, it rules, it guards. Take care, therefore, that you do not stop at a sterile contemplation of God's presence in yourself. Add action to contemplation; to the vision of the divine presence, the faithful fulfillment of the divine will. (421f.; here quoted from Ignatius 1981, 208)

Ignatius Loyola learned and taught spirituality on the basis of his own and his time's presuppositions. Many of these—his theistic conception of God, for example (cf. Sobrino 1978, 414ff.)—cannot be assumed relevant or acceptable today. We can no longer accept some of the interpretations the early Christians gave of their religious experiences either. Even their experiences of contact with the ground of existence may be altogether different from what we—or at least most of us—in modernity are capable of having. But we can still practice an active, creative spirituality. Julio de Santa Ana has pointed out that the single most expressive word in the New Testament for this active spirituality, "this spirituality of the struggle," is *paresia,* which is usually translated "openheartedness" or "fearlessness" [in Danish, literally "free spirit," TH]. Here is what de Santa Ana writes:

> It [the word] appears few times in the Gospels, but is transparent in each gesture and speech of Jesus. His life expresses better than anything else the meaning of evangelical boldness—*paresia.* This is the word used by Luke in Acts 4:13 describing the attitude of Peter and John when they were arrested in order to be tried. *Paresia* is needed to give witness to the word of God (Acts 4:29). *Paresia* is the fruit of conversion, as Paul's experience proves. Since his conversion (cf. Acts 9:20-30) he preaches the Gospel with *paresia* till the end of his life (Acts 28:31). For this, the Spirit sustained him as all other believers—that is the work of the Parakletos (John 16). The normal context of *paresia* is conflict. It is what helps to overcome fear, shyness, weakness. (de Santa Ana 1979, 157 n. 17)

In de Santa Ana's terminology, this free and bold spirit emerges not out of contact with the ground of existence, but from the confrontation with the folly of the cross (cf. 1 Cor. 1:22). It can undoubtedly arise from many other experiences, but for the Christian congregation, at any rate, it emerges from the encounter with the story of Jesus and his death on the cross. It is not something one is born with, or born without. Christian boldness can be learned by training and practice. Kim Chi Ha, a

South Korean Christian, has been able to resist torture and survive many incarcerations in South Korea's prisons primarily because of his familiarity with the meditational techniques of Korean shamanism (cf. Kinnamon 1982). His boldness can stand comparison with Peter's and John's. And as theirs, his boldness was also learned and practiced in the fellowship of a congregation.

Finally, let me just touch on a phenomenon that is not normally associated with manifestations of spirituality, but which nevertheless has more to do with it than one would perhaps believe. I am thinking of *irony*. Irony can of course be nihilistic, as when an ironist ironicizes everything and does not take anything at all seriously. Such an irony, especially when it turns against people's moral and political endeavors to create a better society, becomes reactionary, a veiled defensiveness on the part of the status quo. But irony can also—to use an expression by Jon Hellesnes—be "metaphysical" (cf. Hellesnes n.d.).

Metaphysical irony can be combined with moral and political endeavors, and with the critique of oppressive norms and institutions. But it includes a qualification: it maintains a certain distance, for we could be wrong. We are finite beings and cannot in any way control all the consequences of our actions. That this metaphysical irony—or as we could also say, the irony of spirituality—belongs within the church's praxis after Jesus' death is clear in Jesus' words before Pilate: "My kingship is not of this world; if my kingship were of this world, my servants would fight, that I might not be handed over to the Jews; but my kingship is not from this world" (John 18:36).

If these words are read diachronically, they cannot be taken as historical—the Jew Jesus would not have been able to speak with the Roman Pilate. Perhaps they are intended instead to refer to the Christian church's struggle with the Jewish synagogue (cf. above, chap. 1, sec. 4). But if we read them synchronically and systematically, with an eye to their validity, Jesus is here seen to dismiss the code of the Zealots. And this means that Christian praxis is totally irreconcilable with violence and military power.

If this metaphysical irony belongs within the church's praxis, the Christian community will never identify itself with any other form for political or social praxis—not even the struggle for peace—for its kingdom is not of this world. Even the most moral endeavors can be or become a new struggle for power. Who knows, perhaps that famous priest who said, "Fret not, little children, it might all be a pack of lies," had trained himself in the art of metaphysical-ironical distancing!

4. Contextual Christology

1. The Spectrum of Jesus-Interpretations

Through many centuries now the narratives about Jesus have been retold and reinterpreted again and again. When we talk about Jesus today, our own interpretation of him is not the right, the final, one. Our stories and interpretations are dependent on the cultural and conceptual context that—for better or worse—is ours. We are just as dependent in relation to our social context as earlier generations were in relation to theirs. But it is often easier to see the relativity of previous interpretations than it is of our own. The Western idea of evolution and progress has taken hold of us to such an extent that it is very hard to learn to see ourselves in the same light of relativity as we apply to history.

To illustrate, we can sketch the development of the image of Christ in the Middle Ages. Early in the Middle Ages Jesus was perceived as the Lord who ruled from the throne of the cross, having defeated the evil jailor of humanity, the Devil. Mary was his queen. The drama of salvation had cosmic character and consisted of an ongoing struggle between Christ and the Devil—between the holy angels, on the one hand, and the demons on the other.

In the following centuries interpreters began to put an emphasis on the humanity of Christ. Now the religious drama was seen to take place within oneself and have the character of a journey —a journey toward God. Inner virtues and experiences became more important than the great salvation-historical events. The motifs of atonement, resurrection, and final judgment all tended to fade into the background; the motifs of creation and incarnation became dominant.

In the fourteenth century it was still not Christ the atoner or redeemer that played the central role. The decisive element was the way each individual believer walked by the aid of grace infused through the sacraments, or by way of good works. There were also certain sexually determined interpretations around at the time. Women in particular were devoted to these more human traits of Christ, especially the image of baby Jesus. Women took the lead in urging the public celebration of the Eucharist—"the Festival of the Body of Jesus," as we know, was instituted on the request of women. Behind this concentration on the Eucharist was the sociological factor that women wished to have the same direct contact with the Savior as otherwise had been reserved for the male priesthood. It should not surprise us when we find, in this case among the Cistercians, an interpretation of Jesus as *mother* such as in the following passage:

> My sweet Lord, I gave up for you my father and my mother and my brothers and all the wealth of the world. . . . You know, my sweet Lord, that if I had a thousand worlds and could bend them all to my will, I would give them all up for you . . . for you are the life of my soul. Nor do I have father or mother besides you nor do I wish to have. For are you not my mother and more than my mother? The mother who bore me labored in delivering me for one day or one night but you, my sweet and lovely Lord, labored for me more than thirty years. Ah, my sweet and lovely Lord, with what love you labored for me and bore me through your whole life. But when the time approached for you to be delivered, your labor pains were so great that your holy sweat was like great drops of blood that came out from your body and fell on the earth. . . . Ah! Sweet Lord Jesus Christ, who ever saw a mother suffer such a birth! For when the hour of your delivery came you were placed on the hard bed of the cross . . . and your nerves and all your veins were broken. And truly it is no surprise that your veins burst when in one day you gave birth to the whole world. (Bynum 1982, 153)

Although the passage was written by a woman, Marguerite of Oingt, it was the male-dominated Cistercians that introduced the interpretation of Jesus as mother. At least one element in the social context was the desire of the Cistercian abbots to strengthen their authority, especially among the women, by representing Jesus (and alternately the abbot himself) as mother (cf. Bynum 1982).

We are naturally inclined to write off these shifting interpretations of Jesus during the Middle Ages as having historical or antiquarian interest only: that was the way they interpreted—or could interpret—Jesus at that time. We are interested in the validity of interpretations, and so we must maintain that a presentation of Jesus such as this—in the image of a mother—cannot any longer properly be utilized. But we can also learn from these medieval images of Jesus that every interpretation of Jesus or Christ takes place in a social-historical space and takes color from this particular space. The interpretive context has sociological and (as we have discussed above, chap. 1) political dimensions. Even the practice of calling Jesus "the Christ" is an expression of interpretation. That is why we today must seek to provide an interpretation that corresponds to the conditions, the social space, within which we ourselves live here toward the end of the twentieth century.

But even if we all place ourselves on the same time-axis, namely, in our present age, our social space still differs. We in the Western world all live in modernity. And the main features of modernity, which I attempted to describe in *A Political Dogmatic* by way of concepts such as "abstraction," "futurity," "individuation," "liberation," and "secularization" (cf. Glebe-Möller 1987, 15ff.), are found everywhere in North America and Europe. Nevertheless, the concrete manifestations of modernity in our social space appear different to women than to men, to blacks than to whites in America, to English-speaking Protestants than to French-speaking Catholics in Canada, to devotees of the free market in North America than to Scandinavian social democrats—to mention only a few more or less (though not altogether!) incidental examples. And the differences become even more marked, naturally, when we go from the Western world to Africa, Asia, or South America.

This means that the Jesus-figure is interpreted differently, though within *the same time frame,* in different parts of the world. I have already indicated (chap. 3) that in modern feminist theology the Jesus-figure plays a secondary role—he seems to belong to the patriarchal tradition. To concentrate on Jesus, regardless of the way this is done, is therefore, according to Mary Daly, a kind of Christ cult from which feminists must dissociate themselves (cf. Daly 1973, chap. 3, entitled "Beyond Christology: A World Without Models"). True, as our example from the Cistercians shows, it has also been possible to interpret Christ as a woman, as mother. Reformist-feminist theologians such as Rosemary Ruether can also engage in considerations of the Jesus-figure, because to them he is a partisan representative of all oppressed, men or women (cf. Glebe-Möller 1987, 92f.). Sheila D. Collins utilizes the classical model: Jesus was good enough—it is the church that is all wrong. She writes, "Women throughout the ages have always responded to the simple humanity and dignity they felt Jesus offered them, in spite of official ecclesiastical and civil sanctions against their exercise of this humanity" (Collins 1975, 129). Yet Mary Daly responds, "Jesus was a feminist, but so what?" (Daly 1973, 73). We have thus in the feminist camp not one interpretation of Jesus, but an entire spectrum—and this spectrum is further enlarged when we move on to consider "black" theology and christology.

2. "Jesus Is Black"

At the one end of this spectrum we find for example John S. Pobee of Ghana, who in his book *Toward an African Theology* first gives a rather traditional presentation of "biblical"christology and then moves on to discuss how this christology can be communicated within the Akan society. Pobee thus focuses exclusively on problems of translation. Jesus' relationship to God, for example, can be translated, according to Pobee, with terms drawn from this society's institution of chieftains: God is the chief, and

Jesus is the chief's official spokesman, "who in public matters is as the chief and exercises royal authority, even if subordinated to that of the paramount chief" (Pobee 1979, 94). Just as the chieftain is the tribal sovereign, so is Christ the church's. Pobee's way of posing the problem is rather limited, however. He has not understood that when a christology conceived within Western culture is to be replanted in African soil, or in the third world generally, not only does the linguistic form change, but the content also.

This is clearly recognized by the American black theologian, James H. Cone, at the other end of the spectrum. Even though Cone, when seen through Scandinavian eyes, immediately appears as a conservative, biblically—not to say, fundamentalistically—oriented theologian, it is clear that his christology receives an especially radical formulation because he develops it with conscious reference to the "space" occupied by American blacks. I shall briefly describe some of Cone's main points, as they are expressed in his well-known work, *God of the Oppressed.*

"Who is Jesus Christ for us today?" asks Cone, and he answers with force—and in direct polemic against Rudolf Bultmann, among others—that Jesus Christ is a historical person who lived in Palestine some two thousand years ago. But Cone's interest is not historical-antiquarian (he therefore does not contradict the "textual" interpretation of the figure of Jesus of which I gave examples in chap. 2). His point in claiming that "Jesus is who he was" lies, in the first place, in the observation that the Jesus that the Bible describes was a partisan on the side of the oppressed. It is not, therefore, the Christ of the theological code that Cone writes about. Black slaves could legitimately maintain that slavery is in direct contradiction to the New Testament's Christ:

> They claimed to know about a Christ who came to give freedom and dignity to the oppressed and humiliated. Through sermon, prayer, and song, black slaves bore witness to the little baby that was born of "Sister Mary" in Bethlehem and "everytime the baby cried, she'd a-rocked him in the weary land." He is the One who lived with the poor and died on the cross so that they might have a new life. (Cone 1975, 118)

In the second place, the phrase "Jesus is who he was" means that his humanity is stressed—and with it, that he was a Jew. In the Jew Jesus, the events of the exodus are tied in with the liberation of blacks today:

> Because Jesus lived, we now know that servitude is inhuman, and that Christ has set us free to live as liberated sons and daughters of God. (120)

But Jesus is also "who he is." The crucified one is also the risen one:

> Faith in the resurrection means that the historical Jesus, in his liberating words and deeds for the poor, was God's way of breaking into human history, redeeming humanity from injustice and violence, and bestowing power upon little ones in their struggle for freedom. (120)

As the risen one, Christ is present among oppressed blacks just as he was present with the humble and the weak of Palestine. Jesus was not only a historical person, and not only human. He was, and is, also the divine Christ who transcends the limitations of history precisely by being present in "our" (the blacks') existence today. Resurrection is therefore, says Cone, a political event:

> The politics of the resurrection is found in its gift of freedom to the poor and the helpless. Being granted freedom while they are still poor, they can know that their poverty is a contrived phenomenon, traceable to the rich and the powerful in this world. (125)

And this new knowledge about themselves and about the world means that the poor must fight politically against the social and economic structures that cause their poverty. "Not to fight is to deny the freedom of resurrection" (125).

Finally, Jesus is also "who he will be." Cone accepts his ties—although he is also highly critical—with certain white theologians' eschatological interpretations of Christianity (especially

Jürgen Moltmann's) from the mid-1960s. He demands that the theology of hope take account of and include the oppressed. Otherwise it becomes an ideological justification of the status quo. Black theology has itself always been a theology of hope. Hope for the blacks is not an intellectual idea, but a way in which freedom can be practiced even among those that are oppressed:

> To hope in Jesus is to see the vision of his coming presence, and thus one is required by hope itself to live as if the vision is already realized in the present. (129)

It is in this connection that Cone makes the claim that Jesus is black and that "blackness" is a christological title. For Jesus identified himself with the oppressed, and suffered death on the cross for them (not, as in the theological code, for all people). In the resurrection of Christ, God conquered all oppression and freed all oppressed. But the oppressed today, in America, are the black people:

> Christ is black, therefore, not because of some cultural or psychological need of black people, but because and only because Christ *really* enters into our world where the poor, the despised, and the black are, disclosing that he is with them, enduring their humiliation and pain and transforming oppressed slaves into liberated servants. Indeed, if Christ is not *truly* black, then the historical Jesus lied. God did not anoint him "to proclaim the good news to the poor" and neither did he send him "to proclaim release to the captives and recovering of sight to the blind, to set at liberty those who are oppressed" (*Luke 4:18f.*). (*136*)

Cone has had to bear much for his claim that Christ is black. White theologians have been extremely critical in relation to the concept of "black theology," seeing it as an expression of a political ideology (cf. Holmer 1979, 183ff.). But this notion, in and of itself, should not be so foreign—at least not to those of us who come from Grundtvig's home country! For when Grundtvig tied Christendom and Danishness together, it was in principle the same pattern he followed. Grundtvig did not ever say (at least not as far as I know) that Jesus is Danish, but he could have said so! What Grundtvig could *not* (and would not) have said, of course, on the basis of *his* historical suppositions and *his* context of interpretation, is that it is the identification with the suffering and the oppressed that makes it necessary to say that Christ today must be black (cf. Hoffmann 1983).

Another point is that Cone's black christology rests on a presupposition that we in a secularized modern society like the Danish hardly can share, namely, the fact that the biblical narratives through the centuries—and in part even to this day—have been the only "language" through which blacks in the United States of America have been able to express their experience of suffering and their hope of liberation. Not only is Christ black (Cone characteristically uses "Christ" and "Jesus" interchangeably), but so is Jesus, that is, the Jesus of the Gospels. In a country where blacks have been cut off for centuries from exercising what we now understand to be civil and democratic rights, they have not been able to appeal to, or make their own, the words of the U.S.A.'s Declaration of Independence:

> We hold these truths to be self-evident, that all men are created equal, and that they are endowed by their Creator with certain inalienable rights, that cannot be denied them, among which are life, liberty, and the pursuit of happiness.

Blacks in America have literally had only Jesus to lean on.

Grundtvig, to mention him just one more time, was able to argue on behalf of his liberation program without referring to Jesus. This, of course, applies to an even greater degree to modern attempts at developing concepts of liberty, equality, and justice, such as that of Habermas, for example, by way of an analysis of the presuppositions for successful discourse (cf. Glebe-Möller 1987, 47f.). Cone's christology is therefore—in a double sense—contextual, because it both refers to the social space of American blacks, and utilizes their traditional biblical language (Cone illustrates his point of view throughout with quotations from black music, "spirituals"—as in our first quotation above).

And in Cone's christology, the narratives concerning Jesus'

death are interpreted in such a way as to be miles apart from the theological code. This interpretation contains a spirituality that cannot fail to make a deep impression. It is a creative, active, and acting spirituality that directly involves the praxis of the black churches. Redemption—about which Cone says much—does not consist in a "mystical communion with the divine" or in a "pietistic state of inwardness bestowed upon the believer" (Cone 1975, 229):

> Reconciliation then is not only what God does in order to deliver oppressed people from captivity; it is also what oppressed people do in order to remain faithful to their new gift of freedom. Reconciliation is not only justification, God's righteous deliverance of slaves from bondage; it is sanctification, the slaves' acceptance of their new way of life, their refusal to define existence in any other way than in freedom. (233)

Suffering, therefore, as Cone describes it, is neither in the case of Jesus nor of American blacks a passive suffering—in one sense or another predestined by God, as in the theological code. It is an active suffering, which is aimed at liberation.

The South African theologian Allan Boesak has translated Cone's theology to South African conditions. Boesak differentiates—with reference to one of his countrymen—between "oppressed suffering" and "redemptive suffering." The first form for suffering is a result of violence, and cannot be defended in any way. But the second form for suffering

> is suffering after the model of Christ to save others. This suffering is not an end in itself but is endured in the course of a struggle to realize the well being of others. The power to endure this suffering comes out of love and seeks to realize the objective that lies beyond suffering, namely, liberation. This is the suffering the followers of Christ must bear, but bear manifestly, thereby ultimately serving the liberation of self and the other. (Boesak 1977, 95)

3. Asian Theology

If we move on from black theology to Asian theology, the spectrum of variations is further broadened. Half the world's population, or more, lives in Asia, and about one hundred million Asians profess to be Christian. But these one hundred million are again divided into numerous denominations, many of which vary widely with regard to both age and cultural characteristics. Asiatic theology (and christology) is correspondingly characterized by widely varying orientations. Nevertheless, as the Asian theologian Aloysius Pieris of Sri Lanka has done, one can easily point to certain common characteristics in "the Asian theological sense" (cf. Pieris 1979, 171–76).

The Asian church, according to Pieris, is caught between two theologies that are both of Western origin. One is classical European theology (corresponding to what I have called the theological code); the other is South American liberation theology. One may perhaps wonder why Pieris characterizes the South American liberation theology as "Western European." But in the first place, South American theologians are often educated in Europe, and it is the Western, Catholic interpretation of the Gospels—and of the Gospels' Jesus—that they reiterate. In the second place, it is clear that the Marxist social analysis that they most often put to use, as for example in Gustavo Gutierez's book *A Theology of Liberation* (Gutierez 1973, 21–42, 81–99), is also Western in orientation.

For Pieris there is no doubt that it is liberation theology that means the most to Asian theologians today. Pieris lists five points that are typical of liberation theology. First, it is not simply a matter of explaining suffering and injustice, but of changing an unjust world. Second, praxis is emphasized more than theory: "We know Jesus the *Truth* by following Jesus the *Way*." Third, this way of Jesus is "the way of the cross." The kingdom of God does not emerge automatically in this world, but only through contradiction and struggle. Fourth, the spirituality of liberation theology is not closed up within itself; it expresses itself as solidarity with the poor. And most notably, not in a passive sort of solidarity but a "dynamic participation" in their struggle for full humanity. Fifth and finally, even though the kingdom of God is a gift of God, it is our human obligation to utilize all the possibilities for anticipating it—which leads liberation theologians to a definite engagement with socialism, "i.e., for a definite social order in which oppressive structures are changed radically, even violently, in order to allow every person to be fully human" (Pieris 1979, 171f.).

This theology, in Pieris's estimation, has a relevance for Asians that classical European theology cannot have, allied as it is in actuality and practice with capitalistic technocracy. But since it is Western in origin, even liberation theology does not correspond completely to the social space in which the Asian churches find themselves. Clearly, even in Asian theology, liberation must be central. But liberation is not simply a social concept, it is also spiritual, and must reflect the Asian culture and its "language"—which for Pieris is first and foremost that of Buddhism. Theology is thus not only *words* about God. The wellspring of words is *silence*. It is in silence that God is experienced, while our human needs are articulated in the word. Between silence and word—between Buddhist wisdom and Christian love—there should exist a dialectical mutuality. This is the test of a genuine Asian theology.

In what follows I shall discuss two examples—among many possible ones—of contemporary Asian christology. The first is drawn from the Sri Lanka economist Paul Casperz—one of the most important features of Asian theology is that it is the work not only of professional theologians, but of many laymen and laywomen as well (Casperz 1979, 176–82).

4. Christology in Paul Casperz

Casperz introduces his subject by describing the social and religious situation in Palestine at the time of Jesus: the majority of the population was poor, oppressed in their own land not only by the Roman conquerors but also by their own rich and powerful countrymen. And here it was that Jesus made his choice, a revolutionary choice: to place himself on the side of the poor, the humble, and the outcast. It was in the synagogue at Nazareth that Jesus made this fundamental decision public (cf. Luke 4; we have already seen James Cone emphasizing the same point). Casperz admits that the exegetes may discuss the validity of this or that traditional Scripture passage and the evangelists' own interpretation of them. "But," he says, "our argument does not proceed from this or that text. It is built on the evidence of the accumulation of such records" (concerning Jesus' fundamental choice, JG-M).

Most significant now, according to Casperz, is the recognition that Jesus' fundamental choice implied that he consciously took upon himself the conflict against the power structure. This is clear in the so-called beatitudes, "with its series of powerful subversive paradoxes"; in the judgment scene in Matthew 25; and in the story of the widow's mite, where a poor woman, not the rich benefactors, gives the most valuable offering (Mark 12:41-44 and parallels). It shows up in the parables, "which in traditional spirituality has been used for other purposes, as for example to urge repentance and penance"—Casperz refers, for evidence, to the parable of the prodigal son (Luke 15), which, he says, deals with the father's attempt to get the self-centered older brother to acknowledge that the usual social norms of behavior cannot be applied "in a situation where openness to the dispossessed ought to be paramount" (179).

But even though Jesus was thus a revolutionary, he was so in a different sense than others, because although he sought the conflict and accepted its consequences, he did not stand up against social and religious and political power figures with violence:

> He transcended the way of liberation by violent resistance. He did not reject violence, he went beyond it. By precept and action he showed that there is a more revolutionary way than violence to establish a society of love and sharing of the goods of the earth. (ibid.)

What was this other way? Casperz does not answer this question directly, but he shows in the continuation of his exposition that Jesus was not a Zealot: he did not have the Zealots' confidence in the old social system based on the Torah and the Jerusalem Temple. In place of the Law, Jesus put the freedom of God's children; in place of the Temple cult, the worship of God "in spirit and truth and praxis": in active love of humanity. As Marx did much later, Jesus envisioned a society without estrangement, but unlike Marx he would not utilize the tactics of the oppressors to reach his goal. Typically, the lines from Isa. 61:2 about "the day of vengeance of our God, to comfort all who mourn" are left out of his programmatic manifest in the synagogue in Nazareth.

If one should attempt to pull together the various features of the image of Jesus which Casperz puts into focus, one could say that Jesus transcends the violent approach to revolution because he remained critical in *all* situations. He definitely took the side of the oppressed, but—as, for example, the parable of the workers in the vineyard (Matthew 20) shows—with what I have here called "metaphysical irony." For even among the poor there is sometimes a lack of solidarity. That is why Jesus' life ended on a cross. Says Casperz,

> In a final desperate bid against the revolution, all classes combined against Jesus and killed him. They hoped everything would be over and that society could continue its blunderings again. But Jesus lived on. (182)

Two tendencies, however, have contributed to take the edge off Jesus' message of liberation: first, the hierarchical structure of the institutional church; second, the divinization of his person. Casperz therefore closes with the following paragraph:

> The task of Jesus' followers today is not to live in society according to a belief that Jesus of Nazareth is God. It is rather to live in society according to a faith that God is Jesus of Nazareth. Then the liberation message becomes irresistible and invincible because it is the message, the central message, perhaps the only message, of Yahweh, God of Justice. (182)

Many Western European theologians will probably read the text we have here referred to as a fairly square-pegged piece of liberation theology, perhaps even as political ideology in Christian disguise. There are, of course, both direct and indirect references to Marx here, and the text confirms in that respect Pieris's observations. But one should note also that there is critique expressed, both of Marx and of ordinary revolutionary thought-forms generally. Jesus rejects violence. And if one asks where Jesus and his current disciples find the strength to stand in unceasing criticism of *all* social groups—well, then we are led, as I would see it, back to the via negativa of true spirituality: to its principal reservation in relation to all types of societies and all human structures, or to the silence that precedes the word.

This silence, this wisdom (which in Casperz's case is perhaps more inspired after all by classical Catholic spirituality than by "the Asian mood") is even more clearly expressed by Choan-Seng Song of Taiwan (referred to above, chap. 3, sec. 5). I shall here try to sketch his interpretation of the institution of the Lord's supper, where silence and word, wisdom and love all coexist in dialectic mutuality.

5. Eucharistic Institution in Asian Perspective

Song's interpretation of the institution of the sacrament is developed in chapter 7 of his book ***Third-Eye Theology,*** under the title "The Rice of Hope." The "third eye" is of course a Buddhist concept and stands for the insight into "the nature of our own being," beyond the cloud of unknowing. For Song it means that Christian theology must be willing to see Christ with other eyes than the European—namely, in his case, with Asian eyes, or on the basis of Asian spirituality. In the opening of the chapter, Song recites a Vietnamese poem, "A Mother's Evening Meditation":

> I fill a bowl with new rice
> place ebony chopsticks at the side
> chase the flies away
> and often I see your face as it looked
> the last time you came home.
>
> Today the fields looked ripe,
> the empty rain came back
> spouting black smoke above worn grass.

I filled this bowl to the edge, placed ebony
chopsticks at the side and chased
the flies away. Today is the end
of the month, you would be getting paid today
if you were alive.
You would be going downtown, smoking,
sending postcards home.

I fill the bowl with new rice
look at the pair of chopsticks and your son
just fallen asleep.
A wonderful child, peaceful as a pebble,
he is half a year old now but still has no name.

This is your anniversary.
Suddenly your wife holds her head and cries—
"He died in his spring!"

I fill a bowl with new rice
and sit, noticing the signs of autumn, the fallen leaves. . . .
The child in the cradle smiles at me
I place the ebony chopsticks
chase the flies away
and wipe the streaming tears.
(Song 1979, 142–43)

The ritual that the Vietnamese mother performs, in silence, is an expression of hope. Song comments: "For the mother in the poem the bowl of rice she prepares for her deceased son becomes a link between now and the hereafter, between the present and the future, between life and death. The bowl of rice she fills each day is the symbol and the reality of her faith and hope in eternal life. As long as she lives, she will fill her son's bowl with fresh rice every day. Her son is dead, and she is under no illusion to deny this cruel fact. But in the act of filling the bowl with rice, her son is alive. In the rice that fills the bowl is the mystery of a life that overcomes death. Through that bowl of rice her son is as real to her now as he was in the past. For her that bowl of rice speaks more eloquently than a long difficult discourse on hope. It is the concentration of what it means to live beyond death" (Song 1979, 143).

What is "the Asian mood" in this ritual? In the first place, of course, that it is performed with a bowl of rice, the staple food of Asians. "A bowl of rice carries Asians from one day to another day, from one year to another year, from one generation to another generation." For Asians, rice sustains life from eternity to eternity. That is why the rice that the Vietnamese mother prepares for her dead son can help her remember him. The tyranny of death—regardless of what form it may take—is answered by this Asian woman with a ritual that unifies the living and the dead, all the members of the family.

The rice has thus become "sacramental," or as Song says, "rice is transformed into the power of memory, and the power of memory is the power of life" (144). He develops this perspective—with a reference to Augustine's discussion of *memoria* in his *Confessions* Book 10—in the following manner: When we can no longer remember, it is impossible to conceptualize a life after death. If remembrance ceases, absolute death rules. Or put positively, life is upheld by remembrance, yes, remembrance is life itself. To live is to remember. But remembrance—Augustine shows this—does not create God, it is created by God. God lives in the remembrance. So it is that remembrance becomes the bearer of divine revelation: remembrance has sacramental meaning.

Song is here pointing to a significant theological theme that in our cultural context has been brought to the forefront in the works of Johann Baptist Metz (cf. Metz 1977; 1980, 184–204). Remembrance is of course not the same as memory. This can be seen from the fact that memory—for example, for names or numbers—may fail with the years, while the ability for remembrance may increase. When a person has remembrances—of events in life, of persons he or she has met and that have had influence on his or her life, even when they are long dead—these events and persons are still *alive*. Or, put another way, the less a person is able to remember, the narrower and more self-centered becomes his or her world—in the end restricted to purely physical existence. So, we can say—if only, of course, metaphorically—that remembrance is life. And if we further contemplate that remembrance is precisely something that goes beyond purely physical existence, beyond what a person in a given space and at a given moment in time can experience with the senses—then one can speak with Song about a divine revelation through remembrance, or of "the sacramental meaning of remembrance."

Song then unfolds this latter concept in his exposition of the institution of the Lord's supper. The supper—also known in English as "the last supper"—was literally the last meal, a farewell meal. After the three years the disciples had spent in Jesus' company, it was still not clear to them who he was. Peter would shortly deny that he had even been associated with him. But with the institution of the meal of remembrance, Jesus explains to them who he was, and gives them a way of remembering him as the true Messiah:

> By taking bread and wine and giving them to his disciples with the words, "This is my body," and "This is my blood," Jesus was imparting a sacramental power that would enable his followers to grasp the full significance of his ministry. The memory with which they are to remember Jesus whenever they share bread and wine together will be a sacramental memory relating them to him in a special way. Through that sacramental memory Jesus is not only remembered but is alive. (Song 1979, 147)

This interpretation—with its emphasis on sacramental remembrance—shifts the weight from the theological code's stress on atoning death and forgiveness of sin, and is more reminiscent of Belo's emphasis on that fellowship with Jesus—in his absence and after his death—which consists of "the hands' praxis," namely, the sharing of bread with one another and with the poor and underprivileged. But Song's immediate point is another, namely, that the bread, by way of this sacramental remembrance, becomes identified with the life in Jesus, just as Jesus, according to John 6:30-40, calls himself "the bread of life." Says Song,

> Bread, memory, and life in Christ, these are bound in a sacramental relationship that gives hope, faith, and love. To be caught up in this relationship is to be part of the history filled with redemptive significance. (147)

"Life" is therefore the key word in this interpretation. "What we are primarily concerned about at the Lord's Supper is life, not death" (152). This ties the Christian sacrament in with the Asian mother's daily ritual, for it is life, not death, that engages her. She *knows* that her son is dead, but the bowl of rice symbolizes life and makes her son present for her, not only spiritually but bodily:

> There is an insurmountable gulf separating the living and the dead. But in the communion through the bowl of rice, the barrier between death and life is overcome. It is the living mother and the living son that become united in bodily and spiritual communion. (153)

The cultural-religious background for the mother's ritual appears to be the "ancestor worship" that Christian missionaries have attempted to eradicate everywhere they have gained an entry in Asia. But the Vietnamese mother does not "worship" her son. She does not at all fit into the traditional theological picture in which *religion* is said to represent a search for one's own happiness, and *Christianity* for others'. The mother in the poem simply maintains the fellowship of her family beyond death. That is why her ritual exercise can inspire a new interpretation of the Eucharist, one that penetrates the individualistic Western dimension—the famous Lutheran *pro me*—to the meaning that Jesus himself gave the practice, and which the earliest Christian congregations followed. Song does not develop this critique of the Western or European interpretation of the sacrament the way I have indicated it, but it is surely at the back of his mind when he writes:

> In the experience of the living presence of Christ as we partake of his body through the bread and wine, we ought to be concerned not merely with our own personal relation with him and our own life in him. We experience the living Christ as center of the family to which we belong, a family consisting also of those who have passed beyond this life to another life and of those who are to follow us in the future. . . . The Lord's Table is therefore surrounded by both the visible and

> the invisible members of the great family of God with Jesus Christ at the head of the table. (155f.)

This interpretation of the Lord's supper is closely related to that which I suggested in *A Political Dogmatic,* and on the whole to the concept of the church or the Christian congregation as a fellowship across the ages and generations, even across the chasm of death (cf. Glebe-Möller 1987, 70, 76, 101). But how is the ritual of the Vietnamese mother then related to the Christian Eucharist? Song is apparently still so dependent on Western theology, and on the theological code, that he writes:

> This is the message of the Lord's Supper for countless Asians who prepare the daily bowl of rice for deceased members of the family. In the Lord's Supper they will find the promise and reality of the life they are seeking through the bowl of rice. (Song 1979, 157)

As Song expresses it at this point, the "Asian mood" is now superseded and fulfilled in the Western interpretation of the Eucharist. But in other portions of his book, Song suggests that the followers of Buddha—the "Bodhisattwahs" of Mahayana Buddhism—are "evidence of God's redemptive power and of humanity's hope in the future. They are witnesses to the fact that God has not forsaken the world, that the power of God's love has not been overcome by the demonic power of destruction" (118).

As it appears to me, a truly "contextual" Asian theology or christology would have to be built on some such argumentation as the latter. That is to say, the Vietnamese mother performs an act which points beyond death, and is therefore a "witness to the fact that God has not failed the world"—to remain in Song's rather pathetic style. Even if she had never been acquainted with the Christian Eucharist, she would still have conquered death and created life and fellowship (communion) by her actions. I cannot see how a consistent Asian christology—that is, an interpretation of the Jesus-figure as seen with Asian eyes—could allow itself to maintain that "the realization of that life" which the Asian seeks can only be found in the Christian Eucharist.

The two last quotations concerning the Lord's supper, where Song lets it remain undetermined *who* it is that we or the Vietnamese mother are united with beyond the chasm of death, seem to be dependent on the theological code. Read on the basis of the theological code, it is [first Christ, and through him—TH] everyone. But read from the standpoint of the church's *praxis,* it can only be "the victims," as Dorothee Söelle expresses it (Söelle 1973, cf. Glebe-Möller 1987, 76)—those who suffered and died under oppression or in the struggle against oppression. This Song knows very well, as can be seen in his discussion of suffering.

6. Song on Suffering

Previously in this chapter, I have referred several times to the significance that the interpretation of suffering has been given within the christology of the oppressed. Not least is this the case in Asian theology. It plays a large role in Song's *Third-Eye Theology.*

Song, however, is skeptical in relation to the Japanese theologian Kitamori and toward Jürgen Moltmann, who both seem to allow suffering to take place in deity itself (Song 1979, 59ff.). Instead, Song distinguishes—in quite the same way that Boesak, for example, does—between two different kinds of suffering. There is suffering that is imposed from without and that leads to despair. And there is suffering that God takes on in the crucifixion of Jesus, which is a suffering *together with*—not a substitutionary suffering but a truly redemptive suffering. The latter form for suffering—God's solidarity with us—means that our own suffering becomes "the suffering of hope." When "people" suffer, God experiences it in his suffering—much as the Vietnamese mother does when she each day prepares the bowl of rice for her son. That is what makes suffering into "the suffering of hope" (Song's chapter 8 has the title "Suffering Unto Hope").

In his little book *The Tears of Lady Meng* (1981), Song develops his view of suffering—and also "the Asian mood." Here he retells a popular Chinese legend about the emperor who would build a wall along the northern border of China. But no sooner was one portion of the wall raised before another fell down, and the workers did not make progress. The emperor obtained counsel and was advised to bury one person within every mile of the wall, so every section of the wall would have its keeper. Instead of killing thousands of innocent people, it was decided to bury just one: a man by the name of Wan, which means "ten thousand." Wan was just about to celebrate his wedding when the soldiers grabbed him and led him away. His bride, Lady Meng, was left behind, weeping. Soon she set forth across rivers and mountains to find her bridegroom's remains. When she reached the wall, but still could not find anything, she sat down and wept. And her tears came so strong that the wall was washed away—only Wan's bones were left.

When the emperor heard about Lady Meng, he found her so beautiful that he desired to make her his empress. She accepted his proposal, on three conditions: first, a forty-nine day feast should be held in her dead bridegroom's honor; then the emperor and his entire court should be in attendance at the subsequent funeral for Wan; and finally, the emperor should build a forty-nine foot high terrace by the river's edge, where Lady Meng would bring a sacrifice for her dead bridegroom.

Her wishes were honored, but when Lady Meng ascended the terrace, she cursed the emperor with a high voice for his cruelty and evil—and then leaped to her death. The outraged emperor ordered his soldiers to recover her body, cut it into small pieces, and grind her bones into dust. As they were carrying out the order, Lady Meng's flesh was transformed into a multitude of small, silvery fishes, and in these the faithful soul of Lady Meng lives on forever.

Song interprets the legend as an example of "the people's political theology" (the subtitle of his book). I shall here only point to those elements that have to do with suffering. Suffering and weeping belong together. Tears unify those who suffer. As long as there is weeping and tears, people are able to stand together in protest against all injustices perpetrated upon them. So we must never stop weeping. Because in our tears is that power of love which can cause the great Chinese wall to crumble:

> The source of our political theology in Asia is the people—the people humiliated, oppressed and impoverished. And the power of our political ethic comes from people's tears—tears people shed because of their misery and the misery of others. People capable of crying, people capable of being moved to weep—this is the source and power of our political theology. After all, did not Jesus weep for Jerusalem? Was he not moved to tears by the sick and by the outcasts? That is why we cannot think of the world without Jesus. In a much similar way we can also ask: After all, was not the Buddha moved to tears at the sight of "living multitudes" . . . in misery and suffering? That is why we cannot think of Asia without the Buddha. (Song 1981, 43)

Love is stronger than power. The people's tears are stronger than the naked power of rulers. This, according to Song, is the message of the incarnation: "For God so loved the world that he gave his only Son, that whoever believes in him should not perish but have eternal life" (John 3:16). Even though the powerful rulers may seek revenge and kill their people, not even death can conquer their tears. This is also what the legend of Lady Meng says:

> And imagine again these countless fish, carrying the soul of Lady Meng in them, continuing to shed tears for the injustice done to them, to face authoritarian rulers with the power of love, and to speak the truth in public! Without such little fish, could there be a revolution to change the structures of injustice? (65)

It is of course the resurrection that is interpreted here—in the imagery of the silvery fishes in which Lady Meng's soul lives on. Or as Song says, "Our political theology is located in the space created by the spiritual power of Asian people in suffering" (65f.).

We recognize the notion of the power of suffering and sorrow from the work of the American exegete Walter Brueggemann (cf. above, chap. 1, sec. 6). But Song, on the basis of Asian spirituality, has succeeded in enlarging our understanding of the strength that is contained in suffering—and has thereby presented an interpretation of the New Testament narratives concerning Jesus, his suffering and death, that cannot be allowed to go unheeded in the christological reflections of the Western world. On the one hand, we can learn from these black, South American, and Asian christologies to relativize our own christology, and to realize that it must be developed in the social and historical space and time that are ours. On the other hand, these christologies can show us what is wrong—and what has been wrong—with Western christologies, especially as these have been interpreted, even from the start, in the light of the theological code. And this means also that we must now take up our christological tradition and look at it with new and critical eyes. This I shall attempt to do in the following two chapters, where I first discuss the Chalcedonian formulas that belong to the legacy of the Western churches, and then narrow the scope to one specific phase in the history of the Lutheran tradition.

5. The Two Natures of Christ

1. *Symbolum Chalcedonense*

From the very beginning, what we have called the theological code was given expression in the form of confessions—confessions to Jesus as Lord (Kyrios) or as Son of God. In Rom. 10:9, for example, we read:

> Because, if you confess with your lips that Jesus is Lord and believe in your heart that God raised him from the dead, you will be saved.

Or in Heb. 4:14:

> Since then we have a great high priest who has passed through the heavens, Jesus, the Son of God, let us hold fast our confession.

Gradually, as baptism became the condition for admission into the Christian fellowship, it became the custom that those who were baptized made a confession to Jesus as Lord or as Son of God. This confession became a watchword or countersign (*symbolum*) that documented that one belonged to the church community. And the more the theological code gained credence and authority, the more these confessions or "symbols" were expanded. Three of them—the Apostolic Confession (*Apostolicum*), the Nicaeno-Constantinopolitan (*Nicaeum-Constantinopolitanum*), and the Athanasian (*Athanasianum*) creeds; also identified as the three "ecumenical symbols"—are common to most churches and denominations existing today, and are thus accepted by the Danish Folk church as well.

It is the Athanasian creed that most fully corresponds to the theological code with reference to the interpretation of Jesus. But one of its predecessors is *Chalcedonense,* a christological formula that was adopted at the synod in Chalcedon, near Constantinople, in 451 C.E. (thus, for short, Chalcedon). It goes as follows:

> Therefore, following the holy Fathers, we all with one accord teach men to acknowledge one and the same Son, our Lord Jesus Christ, at once complete in Godhead and complete in manhood, truly God and truly man, consisting also of a reasonable soul and body; of one substance [*homoousios*] with the Father as regards his Godhead, and at the same time of one substance with us as regards his manhood; like us in all respects, apart from sin; as regards his Godhead, begotten of the Father before the ages, but yet as regards his manhood begotten, for us men and for our salvation, of Mary the Virgin, the God-bearer [*Theotokos*]; one and the same Christ, Son, Lord, Only-begotten, recognized IN TWO NATURES, WITHOUT CONFUSION, WITHOUT CHANGE, WITHOUT DIVISION, WITHOUT SEPARATION; the distinction of natures being in no way annulled by the union, but rather the characteristics of each nature being preserved and coming together to form one person and subsistence [*hypostasis*], not as parted or separated into two persons, but one and the same Son and Only-begotten God the Word, Lord Jesus Christ; even as the prophets from the earliest times spoke of him, and our Lord Jesus Christ himself taught us, and the creed of the Fathers has handed down to us.

I shall base my discussion in this chapter on the Chalcedonian formula, because it stands as the final outcome of the christological debates among the early churches and is by far the best expression of that Jesus-interpretation that we have associated with "the theological code." I shall first approach the matter historically, from a diachronic perspective. But the purpose is also systematic: the question will be raised, what validity can we ascribe to Chalcedon in our day? (Cf. my discussion with Jörgen I. Jensen, Glebe-Möller 1983a; my first response to Jensen is incorporated in this chapter.) For Regin Prenter this question causes no problems: Chalcedon will stand guard for the incarnation and defend it against ebionites and docetists, respectively (Prenter 1955, 371; cf. Glebe-Möller 1987, 2). But under a genetic scrutiny, undertaken for systematic purposes, the subject appears a good deal more complicated!

2. The History of Chalcedon

The emperor Constantine, in the beginning of the fourth century, made Christianity the preferred religion in his empire. The Council of Nicaea in 325 C.E. was both the first plenary of the Christian churches and the beginning of Christianity's later status as the state religion of Western Europe. Some fifty years later, in 380 C.E., the emperor Theodosius actually declared Christianity the religion of the state, issuing his famous edict demanding that every man in the realm should confess the apostle Peter's faith, three persons in one deity, just as it was proclaimed by the bishops of Rome and Alexandria. With this the guardians of the Christian faith, the bishops, and the two bishops of Rome and Alexandria out ahead, were put into a conflict-ridden relationship of dependency upon the power of the state, represented by the emperor. As an organization, the church soon imitated the institutions and procedures of the state. This, of course, it could very well do, since it was no longer the congregational fellowship that started out by rejecting all the usual social codes! From the Roman state administration the church learned, for example, to divide itself into separate episcopal "sees." And the periodical gatherings of bishops—the councils—took for their model the deliberations of the Roman senate. From the church, the emperor took the conciliar idea, and used it—for the first time at Nicaea—as a means of adjudicating churchly problems. His position vis-à-vis the church was parallel to his position in relation to the Roman senate (Cf. Grillmeier and Bacht 1962, 1: 96ff.).

But with this the emperor also obtained a unique position within the church. In actuality, it became his task to see to it that the true faith, the Christian faith as defined by the theological code, was formulated and maintained. Church and state were thus infiltrated with each other in a way that we in the modern era can hardly comprehend.

Concerning the invitation to the Council of Chalcedon, the situation was this: the supporters of the theological code were fighting among themselves. There existed any number of christologies or conceptions of the incarnation, manifested not only verbally or in writing, but also in the fact that various theologians and churchmen condemned each other, plotted intrigues against each other, caused each other to be deposed, and so forth. In church-history studies, we quickly become acquainted with Nestorius, on the one wing, and Cyril, on the other. Nestorius was patriarch of Constantinople, Cyril of Alexandria. For Nestorius it was important to keep the two natures of Christ distinct from each other—Mary could thus not have given birth to God (could not be "Theotokos"); for Cyril the opposite was the case. By way of power politics, Cyril drew the longer straw and had Nestorius deposed. What the two of them actually fought about is very difficult to penetrate at this distance. One usually hears that for Nestorius it was most important to maintain the humanity of Christ, while for Cyril it was his divinity that was primary. But both, as we have already said, were followers of the theological code, and were therefore not in disagreement on the point that Christ was both God and man—both, for example, expounded on the passage in John 1:14, "And the Word became flesh and dwelt among us, full of grace and truth; we have beheld his glory, glory as of the only Son from the Father." It was only that Nestorius came closest to the interpretation of Jesus which I have presented above (in chap. 2)—he referred to the scriptural narratives of Jesus' suffering. If it was not the human Jesus that suffered, Nestorius asked, what kind of suffering is it we are talking about?

At the time, the ruling emperor in the East—in Constantinople—was a former general by the name of Marcian. He could not, of course, just sit and listen to all this theological and political strife and polemic, because as God's representative on earth it was his duty to keep peace in the empire. That is why he called the council—and did so against the will of the bishop of Rome, the pope, one might add. Originally, the council was to meet—as it had in 325—in Nicaea. Instead, it decided to convene in Chalcedon, because the emperor was involved in preparations for a military campaign and could not go far from Constantinople. His letter of invitation to the pope in Rome is quite characteristic in its formulations:

> The divine things must be placed ahead of all else. For when the almighty God is gracious unto us, we dare also hope that things are well with our realm and will be still better. Since there seems now to have arisen several points of doubt as regards our true faith, as also the letter of Leo, the beloved bishop in the great city of Rome shows, it has pleased Our Kindness to call a holy synod in the city of Nicaea in Bithynia. There shall, through common consideration and by research of the entire truth, an end be put to certain persons' endeavors, which have recently brought the holy, orthodox religion into confusion. Thus shall our true faith for ever be quite clearly acknowledged, in order that in the future any lack of clarity or division of opinion shall be impossible. Therefore, Your Holiness shall on September 1 be present in the named city Nicaea, accompanied by a fitting number of God-beloved bishops who among the churches that are under Your Holiness' supervision are considered worthy and learned in the orthodox doctrine. But Your Holiness should know that Our Majesty shall also attend the venerable synod, if not by happenstance other official interests such as a campaign shall claim our attention. (Grillmeier and Bacht 1962, 2: 257)

From the line of thought within this writing there runs a straight line to Denmark's Christian IV, 1200 years later! "Piety strengthens the realms" (*regna firmat pietas*), he wrote on the Round Tower—and *he* also had a strong and able hand in guarding the orthodox faith of his realm, as for example when with the help of "his" bishop Resen, he saw to it that the recalcitrant parish pastor Oluf Koch was convicted (cf. Glebe-Möller 1980, 116f.).

The pope, who did not want a council, had to submit to the emperor's will and send representatives to his council (which, by the way, became the largest of the classical councils: at least six hundred delegates were present). In return, the pope hoped to have the council simply adopt certain disciplinary measures against several of the mutually combative theologians and church leaders. But again he drew the shorter straw. The emperor pushed through the adoption of a formula of unity which was designed to make confusion and divisions of opinion impossible in the future.

This formula, currently called *Chalcedonense* (Chalcedon, for short), was worked out by a commission consisting of twenty-three bishops in the presence of an imperial commissioner. The document was on the agenda at the sixth meeting of the council, on October 23, 451. The hopes of the emperor, however, were not fulfilled. Chalcedon did not lead to peace within the church or in the empire—on the contrary, both Nestorius's followers and Cyril's supporters refused to recognize the formula. The Jacobite church of Syria, the Egyptian church, and the churches in Persia all separated from the great Catholic church. And in the longer run, we know, the adoption of *Chalcedonense* ultimately led to the separation of the Roman and Greek churches.

This is just a little of the history of the Chalcedonian formula—and when one is acquainted with it, one can hardly come to any other conclusion than this: we are here faced with a situation so partial and passing as to force us to distance ourselves from it (cf. above, chap. 1, sec. 3). But *Chalcedonense* is still, as we said, the presupposition for *Athanasianum,* and also for Article III of *Confessio Augustana,* the primary confession of the Lutheran communion. So it is necessary that we ask whether Chalcedon, regardless of its origins and independent of its modern interpreters, explains and expounds the figure of Jesus in a way that retains its validity today.

3. The Validity of Chalcedon

The Catholic theologians Hans Küng (Küng 1970; 1987) and Jon Sobrino (Sobrino 1978) have both discussed the validity of

Chalcedon, and have presented us with the following three points of criticism:

The first of these has already been referred to. It has to do with the fact that the Chalcedonian formula did not become, and has never been, a formula for unity. On the contrary, *Chalcedonense* has been a "formula of schism."

The second objection deals with the terminology of the formula, especially in the second part. It is not biblical, but Greek, the critics say, and it is moreover altogether foreign to us today. It talks about two "natures" (*physeis*) and one "person" (*prosopon*), but neither concept has any modern equivalent. The concept of nature has for the Greeks a connotation of matter, material—something that we ourselves have not created but with which we can still do something (cf. "physics"). And the concept of person does not correspond to what we today understand as personal—namely, something like being able to account for one's actions—but is associated in the text with "hypostase" (*hypostasis*), that is, something in direction of "substance" or "being," as in the translation here.

The third objection against the formula's reference to Christ's two natures and one person is, however, the most serious one. It has to do with the absence of any reference—in fact, the inability of the formula to refer—to the historical Jesus (cf. Glebe-Möller 1987, 88). Jon Sobrino writes about this:

> The concepts of nature and person are used to explain the mystery of the Incarnation, but the concept of history is missing entirely. They state that Christ really is true God and true man, but the humanity of Christ is subsumed under the conceptual category of nature. In particular, the formula does not do justice to the humanity of Christ. . . . He was *like* us, but not really *one of* us." (Sobrino 1978, 330f.)

One is used to hearing that the Council of Chalcedon signified a victory for Western theology and for its emphasis on the humanity of Christ. That is only correct if one starts from the fact that Chalcedon's formula itself became a dominant Western doctrinal symbol. Nestorius, after all, continued to be hung out. The insights he had into the reality of the suffering and therefore into the humanity of Jesus were definitively excluded from the formula of 451 C.E. And when the historical perspective is shut out, the theological code spreads itself wide. In the place of Christian community praxis, there appear correct rules of doctrine. But this again means that the humanity of Jesus disappears—only Christ's divinity remains. Presumably, the formula's reference to Mary may be said to contain a historical point of reference. But Mary is here immediately called "virgin," which is to say that it is not Jesus' historical mother about whom the formula is speaking. It is Mary interpreted as *Theotokos* that is referred to here.

Nevertheless, according to theological tradition, *Chalcedonense* was designed to defend the incarnation against the "ebionites and docetists"—the first standing for every attempt to downplay the divinity of Christ, the latter for the opposite attempt to downplay his humanity. Let us take a look at the origins of these concepts.

With regard to docetism, it seems to have been a purely dogmatic-theological concept, without specific historical roots. It does not refer to anyone's self-declaration. One ordinarily refers to Ignatius of Antioch as one of the church fathers who opposed "docetists" most vigorously. But in his letter to the people of Smyrna (found in most editions of the works of the Apostolic Fathers), he does not actually talk about "docetists" but about "the unbelievers" or infidels. These unbelievers were gnostic Christians who with several variations claimed that Christ only suffered and died "in appearance" (*secundum apparentiam*), and such notions Ignatius attacks vehemently. But his interest is not to emphasize the humanity of Jesus. Behind the conflict between him and the gnostic Christians lies the question of the martyrs' death (I am here summarizing the argument in Pagels 1979, chap. 4, "The Passion of Christ and the Persecution of Christians"). If one thinks —as the unbelievers, that is, the gnostic Christians, do—that Christianity is independent of the church as an institution since everyone is in principle able to achieve true perception, gnosis, then it becomes a rather dubious matter to urge martyrdom upon people as the proper imitation of Christ, the way the early church's bishops did. In order to maintain and expand their own authority as leaders of the institutional church, it was important to them that martyrdom was made a matter of salvation. In the blood of the martyrs one could actually *see* the church's presence. Ignatius therefore closes his letter by demanding, in very explicit language, submission to churchly authority. If, in contrast, one ridicules martyrdom, and with it the real suffering and death of Christ—as at least some of the gnostic Christians did—then one can avoid the pressures of episcopal authority. This, in brief synopsis, is what historical-genetic reflection can tell us. And even here the question seems to be a matter of relativity, something partial and passing, from which we do well to distance ourselves.

The matter is quite different in the case of the ebionites. This is a designation that goes back to Irenaeus. He uses the name for a Jewish-Christian sect that had its roots in the church in Jerusalem. And the description is interesting for two reasons: in the first place, it is reminiscent of the fact that the oldest Christian congregation, the Jerusalem church, was actually called *ebjonim,* "the poor." When one reads Rom. 15:25 ("At present, however, I am going to Jerusalem with aid for the saints. For Macedonia and Achaia have been pleased to make some contribution for the poor among the saints at Jerusalem") and Gal. 2:10 ("Only they would have us remember the poor, which very thing I was eager to do"), one can surely get the impression that in the church at Jerusalem there were poor people for whom Paul had assumed responsibility for taking a collection—the church's praxis as charity! But the case was rather that the ancient congregation at Jerusalem understood themselves *as* the poor—those to whom Jesus, according to Matt. 5:3 and Luke 6:21, had promised the kingdom of God.

In the second place the term has connections to those groups to whom—at least according to the liberation theologians' reading of the Gospels—Jesus directed his proclamation and his praxis: the poor, the suffering, the oppressed. To defend the incarnation against ebionites, from this perspective, becomes tantamount to rejecting that interpretation of Jesus which I have exemplified in the previous chapters.

Someone could well object that when theologians today desire to defend the incarnation by way of the Chalcedonian formula, it does not necessarily mean that they give up solidarity with the poor. It is the "paradoxality" of the incarnation that they desire to maintain (so, for example, in Baillie 1948)—and this paradoxality is precisely expressed in the two-nature doctrine, as it was formulated at Chalcedon.

But the question then is, how are we to understand the paradox of the incarnation? Here we return to the subject of spirituality. As we have seen (chap. 3, sec. 2), a Herzel can, for example, interpret Mary as *Theotokos* without thereby becoming a follower of the theological code. To Susannah Herzel, the union of the divine and the human in Mary's body emerges in Mary's *active* answer to the angel. The unity of divinity and humanity is not determined generally, as in "for us and for our salvation," but arises when spirituality becomes active and creative. And if the incarnation is interpreted along these lines, one does not say that Jesus was born "before all time" according to his divinity, and "in these latter days" of the Virgin Mary according to his humanity, as Chalcedon expresses it. An incarnation on the model of Chalcedon's formula can namely, in the last analysis, only become a form for "master mentality"—as every way of thinking must that has lost sight of the difference between oppressors and oppressed and lets salvation be for everyone, regardless. But considered from the perspective of active spirituality, the incarnation—and thereby also the relationship between the two natures of Christ—becomes a symbol of the fact that even as Jesus *became* the son of God, by way of his historical praxis, so can everyone who participates in the threefold praxis of the Christian community also be. This is the perspective that Jon Sobrino so precisely and strikingly expresses when he writes:

> The Son does not simply reveal the potential affiliation of all human beings with God. He also reveals the very process of

> filiation, the concrete way in which human beings can and do become children of God. If Jesus is the Son, then human beings can be children of God. (Sobrino 1978, 340)

In my own view, it is only within the perspective of spirituality that we today can interpret the incarnation, and especially speak of the two natures of Christ. But is it necessary that this interpretation take place in the name of an active, creative spirituality, such as that which Jon Sobrino and the third world theologians on the whole represent? In response, I shall attempt to convey some lines of thought from the North American Catholic theologian Sebastian Moore.

4. Sebastian Moore's Reconstruction

Moore has attempted, in his book *The Fire and the Rose Are One* (Moore 1980), to "reconstruct" with inspiration from Lonergan an experiential basis for the christology that is found in the confessions of the early church, especially Chalcedon. He considers such a reconstruction a theological necessity, *after* liberation theology. Its main features are these:

A. Moore asks, Is there such a thing as a universal human need? He answers in the affirmative:

> The universal human need in its fully adult form is the need "to be myself for another," with the word "for" referring both to my attraction to the other and to the other's attraction to me. (11)

Another formulation of the same need goes like this: "We all desire to be desired by the one we desire." A third expression (and the one Moore especially works with) is simply: "our need to feel significant."

B. This need for significance or meaning—otherwise known in both phenomenological philosophy and sociology as a factor in interpersonal and human relationships—is for Moore a simple fact. When we go beyond the fact and ask why we have this need, and where it comes from, then the question of God arises. Says Moore:

> We are much more emotionally involved with God, or at least with the question of God, than we like to think or to admit. This emotional involvement with God is the key to our self-understanding and to the understanding of religion. It is pre-religious. Religion is the believed-in answer to the unknown other, to the question: "Am I valuable in your eyes?" (26)

Moore goes on to say that the question "Who am I?" is addressed to another. But the only "other" that is able to answer the question is the ultimate reality, which encompasses all being. So it is to ultimate reality that the question "Who am I?" is directed. But directed to this ultimate reality, the question becomes equivalent to asking, "What significance do I have in your eyes?" In this question is contained the question asked of any lover: "Do I have value, meaning, significance, to you?" Consequently, the ultimate reality is also the ultimate lover.

C. Following these reflections, which are built on the well-known notion from traditional spirituality that in love we transcend ourselves and reach out to the very ground of being (cf. above, chap. 3, sec. 4), Moore goes on to define *guilt* (or rather, the feeling of guilt). Guilt is our most important negative feeling. It proves to be the perversion of our most important positive feeling: the desire to be ourselves for another or for others. Guilt (the feeling of guilt) appears, therefore, when "the other" is not attracted to me, and I not to the other (61).

D. But where, in our life, does guilt appear? When is "the other" not attractive to me (or I to the other)? In the situation where my life is experienced as being prey to blind and arbitrary forces. When I am not satisfied with my life, such as it is—that is, beyond my control—with my body, my gender, my sexuality, and all the numberless other things that together make up my given self. Then the relationship between me and "the other," the ultimate reality, has fallen apart (66ff.).

E. This is therefore what guilt means: a ruined relationship. This is also why guilt can only be resolved and cancelled when one rediscovers or reenters a true relationship. In a restored relationship, one or the other of the partners may well have a feeling of low self-esteem, but this feeling recedes in the face of that "true sense of self" which emerges in the relationship between me and "the other" (69).

F. But if guilt consists of, or is, a ruined relationship, there is still another stage of perversion: namely, when the relationship is given up altogether and one pulls back into isolation. This stage is called *sin,* and sin is therefore, according to Moore, the root of guilt and of guilt-feelings (77ff.).

G. Having described the universal need of humans, and the perversions of it, Moore proceeds to reconstruct the christological notion of the early church that Jesus was "without sin." If we first understand that sin is the negative tendency in our life, and not a transgression of divine regulations, then we can see in Jesus our true self and be completely freed of "that cancer which consumes the self." That is precisely what liberation or freedom is:

> First, this freedom is present at the deepest level, where a person confronts the ultimate mystery. There would be a total, unimpeded intimacy with God. . . . Second, this liberated self would be open, in an inconceivably fuller way, to other selves as persons. . . . Third, this liberated self would be so convinced by his God-experience that this was the way life was meant to be, that he would come to see in his life no other meaning than the inauguration of this new, sin-free, guilt-free fellowship of men and women on this earth. (77f.)

H. The disciples see in Jesus their own true self and are gripped by his God-consciousness—itself part of the true self. But Jesus dies. And with him, God dies. But when God dies, so also does the soul's envy of God—Moore refers here, and in several other contexts, to Hegel's famous master-slave dialectic from *The Phenomenology of Spirit.* The point of his interpretation is that the slave does not accept the role of slave, but desires to be master. In the same way, human beings desire to be God or ultimate reality. But when God is dead—as in Jesus' death—no one can any longer have the desire to be God.

I. But then resurrection occurs. Its meaning is this:

> Just as Jesus "buried" God for them [the disciples], so Jesus made God alive again and was the centre of a new God-consciousness. . . . Psychologically there was a displacement of divinity from the old God whom guilt made remote and overpowering, into Jesus. (81)

J. The next step in the development is summarized by Moore as follows:

> Very soon the original God would reappear, and wonderfully so, as the Father who "died" in order to cure our envy of his all-powerful life, and was now seen to have declared his love for us by enacting it in bringing Jesus, our representative, into his immortality. This displacement of divinity from "God" to Jesus would now be experienced as an *extension* of divinity from God into Jesus: God opening up his eternal vitality to us in lifting Jesus out of death to be with him eternally. The extension of divinity from God to Jesus is bewildering and demands a bridge between these two extremes of infinity and humanness in God. That bridge is the Holy Spirit, the life of the extension of divinity. (82)

Sebastian Moore is convinced that with this reconstruction, he has described the experiential background of the early church's christological reflection, of what was meant by saying that Christ was God and man. And he is likewise convinced that we share these experiences with the disciples and the first Christians, and therefore can confess even today Jesus Christ as born of God according to his divinity and born of the Virgin Mary according to his humanity (94–108).

I don't know that he is right. But I have cited him this extensively because he has utilized, in very unique and original ways, the methods of traditional spirituality—references to religious (and protoreligious) experiences—in the interpretation of the early church's christology. And he avoids—as also Sobrino does —the postulate of a presupposed divinity in Jesus. The divinity of Jesus is an expansion of the divinity of God, a transmission of divinity from God to Jesus. On the other side, he has also, especially in the last point, placed himself quite close to the theological code: note that "died" is in quotation marks—God as the ultimate reality can of course not die—and that his entire reconstruction has a tendency toward becoming passive spirituality. Where are the impulses to Christian communal praxis in this reconstruction? Can they be found in any other place than where Jesus' "way" becomes the way of the disciples, then, and of the church, today? Where what Jesus *did* and not what the disciples and the first Christians experienced, becomes decisive?

Moore claims, as I have mentioned, that his project is theologically necessary *after* liberation theologians and political theology and others have put all the emphasis on praxis. Here he is reminiscent of other modern theologians who also, without going back to the theological code and its orthodoxy, attempt to give christology some dimension that transcends the struggle of oppression and solidarity (cf. Charles Davis 1976; Jörgen I. Jensen 1983; cf. below, chap. 7, sec. 5). Moore utilizes Lonergan's thoughtforms. Others take advantage of Frye's concept of metaphor. The central Christian dogmas, according to Frye, can only be expressed in the form of metaphors. He mentions, as an example, the phrase "Christ *is* God and man" or that the body and blood of the sacrament *are* bread and wine. When these and other dogmas are rationalized—as, for example, by way of the assumption of special spiritual substances, or the like—the metaphor is explained. But sooner or later the explanation recedes, and the original metaphor reappears. For "dogmas are perhaps 'more' than metaphor: the point is, they can only be expressed in a metaphorical this-is-that form" (Frye 1982, 55).

It occurs to me, however, that before we cast ourselves upon the metaphors, we have more than enough to do in pulling out the subversive elements in the narratives about Jesus and in interpreting them with a view to the modern context. And in addition, we must learn to use a rational, descriptive language. The perspective of spirituality can keep us aware of the fact that not everything is said by way of our description of oppression or of the church's moral-political praxis. Yet spirituality cannot be a *substitute* for this description and this praxis.

6. Luther's Christology and the Peasants'

1. The Christology in *On the Freedom of the Christian Man*

Luther's conflict with the peasants during the 1520s was also a struggle over the interpretation of the figure of Jesus in the narratives of the Bible. Luther had presented his own interpretation of Jesus already in 1520, in his treatise *On the Freedom of the Christian Man,* a publication that became enormously popular and was called "*the* foundational inspirational writing of the reformation." It was this interpretation with which the peasants a few years later came into conflict, and there is good reason therefore to take a closer look at it.

The original version of the treatise bears the title *Jhesus,* which we may take as indication that it is an interpretation of Jesus we have before us, or at least that Luther wishes the text to be read within a christological perspective—although Luther's reference may well have been, in the style of his times, simply an address or prayer. But Luther does not draw the distinction that we have since learned to make between the "historical Jesus" and the church's Christ. For him, Jesus can only be Christ (or Jesus Christ, Christ Jesus). Or to put it another way, for Luther, Jesus is always the Son of God, the one person of the Trinity who for our salvation came down to earth and suffered the death of atonement. Luther's christology is thus clearly an interpretation of Jesus that has its base in the theological code. The central passage of the treatise is found in section 12:

The third incomparable benefit of faith is that it unites the soul with Christ as a bride is united with her bridegroom. By this mystery, as the Apostle teaches, Christ and the soul become one flesh [Eph. 5:31–32]. And if they are one flesh and there is between them a true marriage—indeed the most perfect of all marriages, since human marriages are but poor examples of this one true marriage—it follows that everything they have they hold in common, the good as well as the evil. Accordingly the believing soul can boast of and glory in whatever Christ has as though it were its own, and whatever the soul has Christ claims as his own. Let us compare these and we shall see inestimable benefits. Christ is full of grace, life, and salvation. The soul is full of sins, death, and damnation. Now let faith come between them and sins, death, and damnation will be Christ's, while grace, life and salvation will be the soul's; for if Christ is a bridegroom, he must take upon himself the things which are his bride's and bestow upon her the things that are his. If he gives her his body and very self, how shall he not give her all that is his? And if he takes the body of the bride, how shall he not take all that is hers?

Here we have a most pleasing vision not only of communion but of a blessed struggle and victory and salvation and redemption. *Christ is God and man in one person.* He has neither sinned nor died, and is not condemned, and he cannot sin, die, or be condemned; his righteousness, life, and salvation are unconquerable, eternal, omnipotent. By the wedding ring of faith he shares in the sins, death, and pains of hell which are his bride's. As a matter of fact, he makes them his own and acts as if they were his own and as if he himself had sinned; he suffered, died, and descended into hell that he might overcome them all. Now since it was such a one who did all this, and death and hell could not swallow him up, these were necessarily swallowed up by him in a mighty duel; for his righteousness is greater than the sins of all men, his life stronger than death, his salvation more invincible than hell. Thus the believing soul by means of the pledge of his faith is free in Christ, its bridegroom, free from all sins, secure against death and hell, and is endowed with the eternal righteousness, life, and salvation of Christ its bridegroom. So he takes to himself a glorious bride, "without spot or wrinkle, cleansing her by the washing of water with the word" [Cf. Eph. 5:26–27] of life, that is, by faith in the Word of life, righteousness, and salvation. In this way he marries her in faith, steadfast love, and in mercies, righteousness, and justice, as Hos. 2 [:19–20] says. (Luther 1978, 286–87)

According to the anthropology that Luther builds on, man consists of two parts, soul and body. The two are independent of each other, but the soul is superior to the body: Luther speaks, for example, of "the inward man," the soul, which the body must be brought to obey (cf. 252f.). If a Christian person believes God's Word, this person's soul is united with the Word, so that all the characteristics of the Word—righteousness, peace, freedom—become properties of the soul (cf. 253). But not only so: faith also unites the soul with Christ as a bride with her bridegroom, and so the properties of Christ become the soul's, and the soul's properties Christ's. This in itself is nothing other than what already happens when the soul believes the Word. For the Word is Christ. Christ proclaimed the Word of God (cf. 254), but he is also himself the Word. Or as Luther expresses it by way of citations from the Gospel of John:

> One thing, and only one thing, is necessary for Christian life, righteousness, and freedom. That one thing is the most holy Word of God, the gospel of Christ, as Christ says, John 11 (:25): "I am the resurrection and the life; he who believes in me, though he die; yet shall he live." (279)

In section 12, however, Luther develops this line of thought further, partly by way of the concept of "the joyous exchange" (*det glaedelige bytte*) and partly by introducing certain concepts from Chalcedon or at least from the christological traditions of the early church.

Christ is both God and man, man who has not yet sinned, and thus, is what humans were before the fall. Because he is both human and divine (has two natures), he can take the sins of the soul upon himself and grant it his eternal righteousness. The soul—the Christian's or the believer's—is thereby set free, and this is precisely that freedom of the Christian which is not affected by any external, bodily circumstances, and which is also—what for Luther appears most important—freedom from having to obtain salvation by good works.

The concept of the joyous exchange is not immediately understandable today. It can be clarified historically-genetically by referring to the efforts of Luther and others among his contemporaries to win what for them was a necessary salvation by performing penitential exercises and "good works" of various kinds: pilgrimages, incantations of saints, sexual abstinence, and much else. There is little doubt that all this activity—for most of his contemporaries as for Luther himself—had the character of exertion, perhaps overexertion, and that it was felt as a liberating experience to know that faith in Christ, in the happy exchange of his work for ours, one is freed from the burden of always having to exert oneself, and is thus set free. But we must ask about its validity today; we must ask: is this concept of a happy exchange valid in a secularized world where we no longer make use of the language of classical christological dogmas and perhaps even no longer are interested in the salvation of souls?

A modern Luther scholar, Jan Lindhardt, discusses this question as a variant of the problem of identity. He argues that any good story is good only to the extent that we can identify with it, and especially with the persons involved. This of course goes for the story of Christ as well. We are "affected" by the story when we hear it, and we are thus identified with Christ—as a bride with a bridegroom—yes, the identification works both ways: we become one with Christ, and he with us (Lindhardt 1983, 95ff., in a passage that focuses on showing that Luther takes over the exemplum-concept of traditional rhetoric).

But the question is then only whether the story of Christ—"the Christ-poem" as Kemp calls it (cf. below, chap. 7, sec. 5)—*can* be a "good" story for us, as it was for Luther. Every teacher has had the experience of telling stories that students simply do not care to hear even though he or she offers all sorts of assurances that they are "good." The distance between the universe of the story and the context of the students can still be so great that they are simply not affected. At any rate, Lindhardt has not offered any proof (what may otherwise not have been his direct intention, either) that Luther's engagement with the Christ-story allows itself to be reproduced in our time.

A more fruitful way, perhaps, is to draw on psychoanalysis. Ejvind Larsen has attempted this with a view to the interpretation of Grundtvig (Larsen 1983, 205ff.). With support from Melanie Klein, among others, he emphasizes how totally little babies are dependent on the love and care of their mother, and at the same time how they must hate the mother because she is never able to totally satisfy all their need for love and care. For she is—precisely as the one upon whom the child is most dependent—also capable of pulling back and leaving the child to itself (regardless of whether she actually does that or not). Caught in this love-hate relationship, the child develops neuroses, as we all do because we have the need for an all-powerful love. But if we were able to have this need satisfied—and this is even more difficult for adults than for children—we would necessarily hate the one who brought us that love. "The happy exchange" would then be the solution to all our neuroses: that is, if in our experience there was a figure who provided love (for Luther: "his eternal righteousness") and *at the same time* took care of our hatred (for Luther: "sin and death").

Looking at it from the psychoanalytic perspective, one could well claim that modern man knows the same problem that Luther and his contemporaries wrestled with. But Luther had a solution to his problem which we do not have: he interpreted Jesus in correspondence with the theological code. Which is to say, he interpreted Jesus not as one who in his life fought oppression and suffering in concrete political ways, by way of his threefold praxis, but as one who sacrificed himself for our sins. And it is this sacrifice- or atoning death-motif that also undergirds his concept of a happy exchange.

Although Luther does not work out the details of the picture, this motif is still evident in several sections of his essay on Christian freedom. One example is section 14, where Luther speaks of Jesus Christ as the high priest who "intercedes for us in heaven before God [and] there offers himself as a sacrifice" (289). Another is section 26, where Luther makes use of the christological hymn from Philippians 2 and writes of Christ that renouncing all and taking the form of a servant, he "suffered and died and did all this for our sake" (303).

A further consequence of Luther's perspective, naturally, is that Jesus' earthly life—his history—totally disappears. For what was it that Jesus "did"? It was only to preach God's Word, that is, himself as the one in whom sin and death are conquered: thus Christ is not the one who heals the sick, feeds the hungry, and stands in solidarity with the oppressed. No, for Luther it is definitively established that "Christ has not come for any other ministry than to preach the word of God" (cf. 254). This is why the kingdom, which Christ shares with his believers, is also for Luther (only) a spiritual kingdom, indifferent to any form of oppression —if oppression is not otherwise made into an outright gain with respect to eternal happiness or Christian freedom:

> The power of which we speak is spiritual. It rules in the midst of enemies and is powerful in the midst of oppression. This means nothing else than that "power is made perfect in weakness" [2 Cor. 12:9] and that in all things I can find profit toward salvation [Rom. 8:28], so that the cross and death itself are compelled to serve me and to work together with me for my salvation. This is a splendid privilege and hard to attain, a truly omnipotent power, a spiritual dominion in which there is nothing so good and nothing so evil but that it shall work together for good to me, if only I believe. (290)

This does not of course mean that the Christian is not also obligated to do works of charity in relation to the neighbor—Luther uses Philippians 2 precisely to underscore this responsibility. But faith in Christ and his work of atonement comes first and has priority. Whatever good deeds, whatever moral or political praxis that may here be in the picture—it is all left undefined except for the device that "a good tree bears good fruit." As Luther writes to Johannes Bugenhagen in his copy of *On the Freedom of the Christian Man:* "You have asked that I should prescribe for you the proper way to live. The true Christian has no use for moral prescriptions. For the spirit of faith guides him in all that God wills and the love of neighbor requires. Therefore, read this. Not everyone believes the gospel. Faith is sensed (sensitur) in the heart" (Bugenhagen 1888, 8). In actuality, this means that Christian praxis draws its content from the ordinary "worldly" morality—as can be seen, for example, in Luther's catechisms, especially in the exposition of the Ten Commandments.

For the peasants, of course, the matter stands in an altogether different light, as we shall see.

2. The Peasant Uprising and the *Twelve Articles*

The uprising of the peasants in the sixteenth century is ordinarily—that is, among theologians—considered a movement altogether different from the reformation that Luther headed. Back when I was a student, we learned in church history that the Peasant Revolt was "primarily an economic, not a religious movement." It was pointed out that these were Roman Catholic farmers that rose in protest—and in those areas of the German empire where Luther's thoughts had found the least acceptance. Behind these perceptions stands an old Lutheran tradition. In Denmark, it was underscored already by Hans Tausen that Luther had no responsibility in the uprising. His opponent, Poul Helgesen, naturally maintained the opposite (cf. Tausen 1870; Helgesen 1932, 26ff.; for Tausen it was of course important to cleanse Luther and the Lutheran Reformation from all suspicion that it could be socially destructive, while for Helgesen—representing "the old church"—the aim was the opposite).

It is of course quite misleading to distinguish between economic and religious matters the way my church-history textbook did (cf. Holmquist and Nörregaard 1949, 69ff.; even in Leif Grane's work, Grane 1968, 192ff., this differentiation continues: "the peasant war was not a religious conflict," but "first and foremost a struggle for the autonomy and social rights of farmers"). Such a distinction is typically modern; it did not exist at the time of the Reformation (although Luther's differentiation between the worldly and the spiritual "regiments" contributed to clearing the way for it). The worldview of the time was religious. People thought and spoke and analyzed things in terms of religious categories, that is, in categories drawn from the biblical writings. This was so, naturally, also among the peasants.

And even though Luther cannot be held directly responsible for the peasant uprising, there is no doubt from a historical perspective that his emphasis on Scripture and his references to the gospel played an important role for the peasants.

Nonetheless, the roots of the Peasant Revolt go quite far back. Time and again in the late Middle Ages the poor landless farmers rose up against the landed gentry—and even against the monasteries. In Alsace, for example, where the farmers were constantly confronted with the practice that when their harvest was good, the grain was stored in the monasteries' barns, and when the harvest was slim and the lower quantities should have created greater demand and higher prices, the monasteries dumped their grain reserves onto the market and the farmers were left, as usual, with little or nothing (cf. Rapp 1975). In the German regions, we know of any number of uprisings under the symbol of the peasant's clog (the so-called *Bundschuh* movement). Several of them were well organized and had the character of true mass movements. Yet the largest uprising of them all was the one that took place in 1524–26, in four different centers of southern and central Germany, and in Austria and Tyrol (here and in the following, my presentation of the peasant uprising is based on van Dulmen 1977).

It is not possible to identify any single thing as the reason for the uprising. Increased parceling of land, unemployment, rising prices, higher cost of living, and a steady increase in the spread of serfdom are all among the candidates. But the most decisive factors seem to have been, first and foremost the new sovereign states that installed a centralized bureaucracy and Roman jurisprudence, and thus robbed the peasants in the villages more and more of their customary and traditional rights. In the *Twelve Articles* (Luther 1967, 8–16), sections 4 and 5 deal graphically with the characteristic complaint that while a poor man up to now had been permitted to hunt and fish and gather firewood in the forests, this the authorities and the nobility had now forbidden, which appeared to the peasants "unseemly," "unbrotherly," "selfish," and "not in accordance with God's word" (12–13). In the second place, it is clear that precisely the reformers' preaching served to strengthen the peasants' self-consciousness and sharpen their demands for reform.

On the whole the Peasant Revolt was based upon *der gemeinde Mann*—"the common man"—and primarily the common man in the country. But several towns joined the movement as well—and the movement's spokesmen were often theologians and other men considered highly educated for their time, such as princely secretaries.

The uprising manifested itself in such a way that the peasants in each of the aforementioned locations joined together in organized leagues, and these increasingly were aimed toward real change in the structures of society. The goal was thus no longer simply to defend the old rights or the old customs; the leagues soon began, in varying degrees and with differing formulations, to demand equality and societal democracy in general. The farmers of Franken, for example, said that "what the holy gospel establishes shall be established, and what it abolishes shall be abolished." Consequently, no one shall any longer pay the lords any tithes, rents, or fees, until it has been determined by the learned what is justly owed the ecclesiastical and secular authorities, and what is not. Likewise, oppressive palaces and castles that have caused difficulties for the common people shall be demolished or burned. All authority, ecclesiastical or secular, noble or nontitled, shall follow and hold to the tenets of the common law of citizens and farmers, and no one shall count for more than the common man does. As the farmers of the Black Forest demanded, the people of each area should come together, form a league, and create "an order after the word of God." Palaces and castles should be done away with. And so on.

The articles and proclamations that the peasants set forth vary widely in detail. But if we turn to the *Twelve Articles,* which were formulated by the farmers on Schwaben and distributed most widely within the movement, we can get an idea as to what the uprising was all about. The starting point, as already stated, was the defense of the old rights. One point, beyond those already referred to, was that the farmers were to have permission to retain access to the common lands, the public pasture. Serfdom was to be opposed, as was, generally, all tyranny—including taxes and tithes—on the part of the landed gentry. On the whole, the idea behind these rather moderate demands was not to abolish all authority or nobility—we are still a half-dozen years away from the real anarchists of the reform movement, the Anabaptists. But government is not beyond criticism, and subservience to it is no longer absolute. Some of the articles have a purely "churchly" aim—and here, of course, one can easily hear echoes especially of Luther's thought—as when Article 1 immediately demands that the parishes themselves shall have the right to elect and depose their priests. The article continues:

> The pastor whom we thus choose for ourselves shall preach the holy gospel to us clearly and purely. He is to add no teaching or commandment of men to the gospel, but rather is always to proclaim the true faith and encourage us to ask God for his grace. He is to instill and strengthen this true faith in us. For if the grace of God is not instilled in us, we remain mere flesh and blood. And mere flesh and blood is useless, as Scripture clearly says, for we can come to God only through true faith and can be saved only through his mercy. (10)

3. Luther's Critique of the *Twelve Articles*

One should have thought that this last demand was fully harmonious with Luther's thoughts. In his pamphlet *A Peaceful Appeal on the Occasion of the Schwabian Peasants' Twelve Articles* (Luther 1967, 17–43), Luther also declared that "this article is just only if it is understood in a Christian sense, even though the chapters [of Scripture] indicated in the margin do not support it" (37–38). Luther's commentary to Article 1 deals with "a Christian and evangelical way to choose and have one's pastor" (ibid.). And it proves to consist in this: if the authorities will not give the congregation the parish priest the members have requested, then the congregation must itself secure his support, and if the authorities still will not recognize him, "then let him flee to another village, and let those who so desire flee together with him, the way Christ has taught us." Luther has surely hit his aim with these specifications. But there is nothing in the article at hand to indicate that the peasants intended to ask permission of the authorities, whether when the priest was to be elected or —"if he behaves himself improperly"—deposed. Their ideas concerning the free election of priests were far more radically democratic than Luther could ever realize or accept.

But again, the secular and the Christian are not at all separated in these articles. The "christianly" has worldly consequences. Quite characteristic is the fact that every article—as Luther's reply also indicates—was trimmed with Scripture passages, and that references to Scripture are used again and again as arguments for what we today would consider purely secular or even economic demands. Article 4, for example, which deals with the rights to free hunting and fishing, refers in the margin to Genesis, and in the text itself to God who, "when he created man, gave him the power over all animals, over the birds of the air and the fish of the water" (Luther 1967, 10–11). In actuality, the thoughts set forth here are quite deep—and definitely not without relevance today. When Genesis 1 states it this way, and as the farmers write it (or more correctly, their penman, the lay preacher and furrier's apprentice Sebastian Lotze), is it not necessarily a contradiction of Judeo-Christian creation faith to exclude some people from those rights and privileges that God has given to *all humankind?* Or oppositely, to reserve those rights that God has given to all for only *some* or *a few?* The American Catholic scholar Michael H. Crosby has interpreted this text in a way that seems to me both very pertinent and in full correspondence with the peasants' point of view back then. He writes:

> All people in creation have the right of access to the resources of the earth that they need in order to live in dignity as images of God. Correspondingly, each person has the duty (since we are to live in community) to enable all other people to have access to the resources they need to lead dignified lives. (Crosby 1977, 28)

Luther adds no commentary to this particular article (or to most of the rest, for that matter). He refers to himself as "only a preacher of the gospel" and passes the matter to the jurists (Luther 1967, 249f.)—though when it suited Luther's purposes, he could also claim the right of preachers to deal with juridical or economic questions, even from the pulpit! (Cf. Frostin 1983, 108f.). But on Article 2, Luther makes stern commentary. In this article the farmers say that even though the tithe is an Old Testament provision that is abolished by the New Testament, they are prepared to continue paying the tithe of grain. But the tithe is to be divided between the priest and the poor, and the surplus is to be stored with a view to periods of famine or need, "so that no general tax shall be laid upon the poor" (Luther 1967, 11). For Luther, this is altogether unacceptable: "This article is nothing but theft and highway robbery. They want to appropriate for themselves the tithes, which are not theirs, but the rulers', and want to use them to do what they please. Oh, no, dear friends! That is the same as deposing the rulers altogether. Your preface expressly says that no one is to be deprived of what is his" (Luther 1967, 38). If one wants to give anything away, it must be one's own!

Again Luther has doubtlessly hit his mark. The farmers must have thought that they themselves had the right of ownership to the fruits of their labor and that they could dispose of their grain by common consent and without interference from the authorities. Indirectly, they thereby removed the foundations of the feudal society in which they lived—and to which, in Luther's view, one could not even imagine there being any alternative. But the conflict between Luther's conceptions and the peasants' reaches its high point only in reference to Article 3, where the peasants explicate their interpretation of Christian freedom as follows:

> Third, it has been the custom for men to hold us as their own property. This situation is pitiable, for Christ has redeemed and bought us all with the precious shedding of his blood, the lowly as well as the great, excepting no one. Therefore, it agrees with Scripture that we be free and will to be so. It is not our intention to be entirely free. God does not teach us that we should desire

> no rulers. We are to live according to the commandments, not the free self-will of the flesh; but we are to love God, recognize him in our neighbor as our Lord, and do all (as we gladly would do) that God has commanded in the Lord's Supper; therefore, we ought to live according to his commandment. This commandment does not teach us to disobey our rulers; rather to humble ourselves, not before the rulers only, but before everyone. Thus we willingly obey our chosen and appointed rulers (whom God has appointed over us) in all Christian and appropriate matters. And we have no doubt that since they are true and genuine Christians, they will gladly release us from serfdom, or show us in the gospel that we are serfs. (Luther 1967, 12)

The article has to do with serfdom, which the peasants reject except that it can be proven from Scripture that they shall not be free but bound. Scripture is here as always their highest norm. Their reason for rejecting serfdom is itself drawn from Scripture: from the Christ-story of the New Testament. The farmers remain formally in tune with the theological code: Christ has liberated and redeemed us all with his precious blood. But they break out of it also. In the same way as James Cone and the black theologians four and one-half centuries later (cf. above, chap. 4, sec. 2), they hear in the narratives of the atonement a message of concrete liberation: when Jesus is said to have bought our freedom, we are all free. Not only in a form of freedom that relates to the soul, but bodily freedom. This does not mean anarchism; authorities are still to be acknowledged. But it means that we are set free for a new praxis, in which we acknowledge God in our neighbor and do all that God has commanded us in the sacrament. A marginal reference to Luke 6 shows that the farmers must have thought—among other things—of these words:

> But I say to you that hear, Love your enemies, do good to those who hate you, bless those who curse you, pray for those who abuse you. To him who strikes you on the cheek, offer the other also; and from him who takes away your coat do not withhold even your shirt. Give to every one who begs from you; and of him who takes away your goods do not ask them again. And as you wish that men would do to you, do so to them. (Luke 6:27ff.)

But is it not precisely words like these (or similar passages) that the peasants do *not* live by, when they make an uprising and take their masters' property away from them? And is not Luther right when he criticizes them? The question is of course twisted, for the peasants do not distinguish—as Luther does—between their own rights and those of their masters. The Christian way to act is what we have all learned from God (Jesus) in the sacrament, the farmers say, and they apparently mean (just as later Belo, cf. above, chap. 2, sec. 2) that Jesus at the institution of the sacrament taught his disciples the praxis which was to be theirs after his departure. This praxis consists in a communion of bread and property. If such words as those about loving one's enemies had been directed to their masters and overlords, the assumption would have been that the masters were outside the fellowship of the Christian community. But that is clearly not the peasants' assumption. They presuppose, to the contrary, that their masters are subject to and bound by the words of Jesus, just as they themselves are.

The farmers do not just draw concrete and social consequences of their interpretation of the story of Jesus, but they demonstrate also that they interpret it as the church's praxis. This is in full agreement with the fact that the preface of the *Twelve Articles* speaks not only—as Luther does—of Jesus as the proclaimer of God's word, but explicitly says that the gospel is "a message about Christ, the promised Messiah, whose words and life teach nothing but love, peace, patience and unity. And all who believe in this Christ become loving, peaceful, patient and agreeable" (Luther 1967, 9). For the farmers, it is a matter of "hearing the gospel and living according to it" (Franz 1963, 175, 4ff.). When Luther on his side spitefully rejects the farmers' utilization of Scripture, it is not because he believes himself to be—in an academic sense—more knowledgeable in the Scriptures, but because he interprets them exclusively according to the theological code. The farmers, however, are primarily hearing them as a story concerned with the church's praxis.

It is obvious that Luther's reaction to Article 3 had to be violent. He writes:

> You assert that no one is to be the serf of anyone else, because Christ has made us all free. That is making Christian freedom a completely physical matter. Did not Abraham [Gen. 17:23] and other patriarchs and prophets have slaves? Read what St. Paul teaches about servants, who, at that time, were all slaves. This article, therefore, absolutely contradicts the gospel. It proposes robbery, for it suggests that every man should take his body away from his lord, even though his body is the lord's property. A slave can be a Christian, and have Christian freedom, in the same way that a prisoner or a sick man is a Christian, and yet not free. This article would make all men equal, and turn the spiritual kingdom of Christ into a worldly, external kingdom; and that is impossible. A worldly kingdom cannot exist without an inequality of persons, some being free, some imprisoned, some lords, some subjects, etc.; and St. Paul says in Galatians 5 that in Christ the lord and the servant are equal. My good friend Urbanus Rhegius has written more adequately on this subject. If you want to know more, read his book. (Luther 1967, 39)

Luther's reaction is consistent with the christology that forms the basis for *On the Freedom of the Christian Man*. For the most part, he simply repeats its main features. The lordship of Christ is a spiritual kingdom; the freedom of the Christian is a freedom of the soul and can therefore be present even though the body is unfree. The only new feature is that Luther so directly links freedom and unfreedom in the existing feudal society with equality and freedom in Christ's spiritual kingdom. One can interpret Luther's political philosophy of inequality as an expression of his historical limitations—"it was the way one had to think in Luther's time." But the peasants were able to transcend these limitations! So it may be more correct to say that Luther's argumentation, in this case as in other places, shows how an interpreter's political standpoint, then as now, interacts with his or her interpretation of the figure of Jesus. One who accepts a society of inequality and oppression, and who interprets the Jesus-figure on the basis of the theological code, will have no interest in Jesus' concrete praxis. And vice versa: if Jesus is interpreted from the viewpoint of the theological code, the church's praxis will become subject to the currently dominant social codes.

In Luther's case, this does not mean that he could not also criticize the princes or rulers just as sharply as he criticized the peasants. But his interpretation of the figure of Jesus provided him, in the last analysis, no other possibility than to put himself on the side of the rulers, and against the peasants. Thus Luther gave his blessing to their drowning the rebels in blood. We have the following story from an officer describing the behavior of the Margrave of Brandenburg:

> Shortly thereafter he went up into the hills in order to crush the rebellion there. Master Augustine, the margrave's herald, has proof that he (Augustine) beheaded eighty during this campaign, namely, one in Neuhof, one in Erlbach, ten in Ipsheim. . . . In Leutershausen he chopped the fingers off seven. In Kitzingen he put out the eyes of sixty-two, and so on. On application, he had been promised one guilden for each beheaded and one-half guilden for each blinded or maimed. . . . Summa summarum 114.02 guilden. (Zschäbitz 1967, 204f.)

And so it is ultimately up to each of us individually to decide with whom we will identify in the story of the Peasant Revolt!

7. Christology Today

1. The Inevitability of Contextuality

A modern christology must be contextual, for at least two reasons. In the first place, we know today that any interpretation—and therefore also the interpretation of the figure of Christ in the New Testament—takes place within a given interpretive context, one that is determined by the social context within which the interpreter finds himself. Within this context, of course, we also find everything that we—somewhat indefinitely—include within the cultural tradition: all the codes with which we have become familiar through upbringing, schooling, reading of newspapers, and much else. Indeed, we are enculturated to such a degree that only some altogether extraordinary happening or circumstance will enable us to discover and identify these codes.

And in the second place, it is no longer possible to claim to those in other parts of the world that the Western interpretation of Jesus, which for almost two thousand years has been identical with that of the theological code, is the only correct or possible one. It is this that we in recent years have learned from the third world—as I have exemplified in Chapter 4—when its theologians raise the just demand that the interpretation of Christ *there* happens within a black or South American or Asian context (and we could of course mention many other contexts as well). To ignore or overlook this demand altogether is really nothing more than pure Western imperialism in the name of Christianity.

This means that we in Western Europe—or perhaps especially in Denmark—must now develop a christology for advanced industrialized society, and on the basis of our, that is, modernity's, conditions. In Denmark, we must—to reinforce this point—claim that "Jesus is Danish," just as James Cone on the basis of his presuppositions must claim that "Jesus is black." On the surface, however, such a contextuality seems to make any kind of conversation concerning Jesus between a Dane and an American black or a Taiwanese altogether impossible. We end up with a whole series of contextual christologies, each with its limited and relative validity.

But the case is more complex than that. It is not so simple as to say that they have their christology and we must have ours. At least four arguments speak against such a simplification:

First, even the interpretive context of a black in the U.S. or in the Caribbean, or even of an Asian, is decisively characterized by modernity. It could be—yes, it could hardly be otherwise—that modernity in its concrete socioeconomic form, namely, Western technocracy, goes against what we have called the Asian mood, and that therefore, an Asian christology must be worked out in direct contradiction to modernity. But even in that case, modernity is still an inevitable factor for the Asian interpreter.

Second, there are also essential parallels between the Western European context and the contexts of the third world or of blacks in America. Here, as there, oppression characterizes social structures—if these structures are not in themselves implicitly oppressive. There is still an uncomfortably relevant truth to Marx's and Engels's statement in "The Communist Manifesto":

> The history of all hitherto existing society is the history of class struggles.
>
> Free man and slave, patrician and plebeian, lord and serf, guild master and journeyman, in a word, oppressor and oppressed, stood in constant opposition to one another, carried on an uninterrupted, now hidden, now open fight, a fight that each time ended either in a revolutionary reconstitution of society at large or in the common ruin of the contending classes. (1959, 7)

In contemporary Western Europe, the oppressed are perhaps for many reasons, historical and social, more difficult to catch a glimpse of than in Marx's and Engels's rather schematic rubrications. We are all subject to "the system's coersion" or to its "colonization of our life-world" (Habermas's terms, cf. Glebe-Möller 1987, 54). But some people experience this more than others. In his book *At the End of the Table,* Henning Friis described, as late as in 1981, those groups that are especially vulnerable in modern Danish society (Friis 1981; he counts the disabled, old-age pensioners, long-term welfare recipients, single mothers, immigrant workers, and the homeless—"the ragged proletariat"). And between these groups and the oppressed farmers or farm-workers in South America, the difference lies simply in the degree of explicit violence to which they are subjected.

Third, we here in the Western world—Europe and North America—have at least this in common with the rest of the world: that we interpret the same text—the Bible, and especially the New Testament. We do this out of different linguistic presuppositions, which are part of our respective "codes," but the text itself sets certain limits to the interpreter's area of operation (cf. above, chap. 1, sec. 7). And certain limits thereby arise regarding how relative a christology can be.

Finally, in the fourth place, spirituality—even in the form of metaphysical irony—means that that which at any given moment and in any given place is presented as an adequate christology must nevertheless not be considered so. Or in other words, that we must acknowledge that Jesus as the "object" of our wishes and our political strategies withdraws—and therefore forces us to start all over again. Only a passive spirituality gives up any attempt to develop christology contextually!

2. The Crucifixion

It is usual to consider the resurrection the central theme in the New Testament's narratives concerning Jesus. But the resurrection has the crucifixion as its presupposition or foundation. Even though Paul to some extent interpreted Jesus on the basis of the theological code, his letters also show that he was very well aware of the decisive importance of the crucifixion. To the church at Corinth he wrote: "For I decided to know nothing among you except Jesus Christ and him crucified" (1 Cor. 2:2). The statement follows a historical-systematic argument, where the central passage is this:

> For since, in the wisdom of God, the world did not know God through wisdom, it pleased God through the folly of what we preach to save those who believe. For Jews demand signs and Greeks seek wisdom, but we preach Christ crucified, a stumbling block to Jews and folly to Gentiles, but to those who are called, both Jews and Greeks, Christ the power of God and the wisdom of God." (1:21–24)

We can describe this way of thinking in the following semiotic quadrangle:

S 1 The world's wisdom — God's wisdom S 2

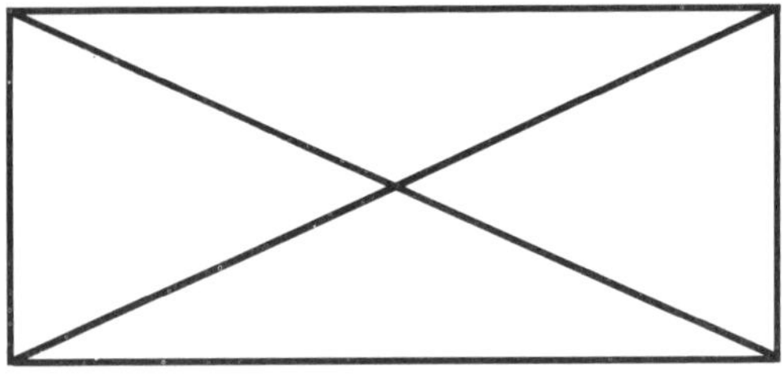

– S 2 The scandal — The crucifixion – S 1

In direct contradiction to the world's wisdom stands God's wisdom. According to the world's wisdom, that is, the current social codes, it is power and social status that count. The more power and the higher the social status, the closer one is to happiness ("salvation"). To place the crucifixion at the foundation of salvation stands in glaring contradiction to this code. This is why the *scandal* is "implicit" in the world's wisdom, while in God's wisdom the crucifixion is directly implicated.

But how can the crucifixion obtain such central placement? Is it capable of being held together with naming the stories of Jesus—and within these stories, Jesus' own message—an "evangel," a good and happy message? One way to address this problem is of course to read or interpret the crucifixion in correspondence with the theological code. It then becomes Jesus' predetermined death—as we have already discussed (above, chap. 2, sec. 6). But if we cannot accept this reading because it does not leave room for—perhaps it even directly contradicts—Jesus' partisanship on behalf of the poor and oppressed, then we are apparently left with a crucifixion that is nothing less than the *murder* of Jesus. A murder that he perhaps could have predicted, but that at least was not willed by him—for that matter, no murder can be. In the garden of Gethsemane, he prays that the cup pass from him, that is, that he should not lose his life in the confrontation with the Jewish and Roman rulers (cf. Mark 14:36). And on the cross he cries: "My God, my God, why hast thou forsaken me?" (15:34). But can a modern reader or hearer learn anything from this, other than the sad word that whoever sets himself against the dominant social codes, or against the powerful in society, is bound to be destroyed by them?

At first glance the answer must be: no! That is precisely the message, and it is not a good and happy one at all. On the other hand, this is still, of course, an important message to Jesus' followers—to the church community. For it says: you must be prepared for the cost. If you follow after me—in the praxis of love, faith, and hope—you must know the price: those in power will turn against you and crucify you. And again, conversely, the church can learn that when it experiences progress and success in this world—that is, among those in power—its praxis is beginning to tarnish. For it has begun to accommodate the current lay social codes.

We can still go a step further, however, if we reflect upon what Cone, Song, and many others emphasize: that even though Jesus himself did not will his own death—did not wish to be murdered—he did, according to the narratives in the New Testament, accept his crucifixion as a consequence of his partisanship for the poor and the weak. He did not command his servants to come out fighting for the good cause; he commanded one of his followers, in the Gethsemane garden, to put his sword back in its sheath (Matt. 26:52), just as he had consistently rejected a leadership modeled after the Zealots. He had, as it is stated briefly in Mark 1:12 and elaborated in mythological language in Matthew 4 and Luke 4, refused the devil's or Satan's temptations:

> Again, the devil took him to a very high mountain, and showed him all the kingdoms of the world and the glory of them; and he said to him, "All these I will give you, if you will fall down and worship me." Then Jesus said to him, "Begone, Satan! for it is written, 'You shall worship the Lord your God, and him only shall you serve.'" (Matt. 4:8ff.)

And when Jesus, according to Mark 8:31, had for the first time predicted his coming suffering and death, and Peter—who even here thinks in accordance with the codes of this world—begins to scold and correct him, Jesus refuses Peter the same way he refused the devil: "Get behind me, Satan! For you are not on the side of God, but of men" (Mark 8:33). It is quite correct, as a matter of fact, when many early manuscripts consider the temptation narrative in Matthew 4:8ff. in the light of Peter's rebuke, and vice versa, and thus employ the same phrase in both contexts: "Begone," "Get behind me, Satan!"

With his rejection of the ways of power and force, Jesus positioned himself in solidarity with the oppressed. It is in further development of this solidarity-motif that we find, in 1 Peter 3—and still in mythological language—the reference to Jesus "being put to death in the flesh but made alive in the spirit; in which he went and preached to the spirits in prison . . . " (vv. 18f.). Quite apart from the exegetical problems involved in this obscure statement, it must mean that Jesus, in his death on the cross and therefore also beyond his death, shows himself in solidarity with all those who have gone to their grave in the hell of oppression. That is also why these descent- and inferno-themes became so important in the early church and during the Middle Ages. As it is expressed in Grundtvig's rendition of an Old

English poem, with his descent into hell Jesus "muffled the weeping" and "freed the devil's prisoners":

> Tonight there were knocks on the gates of hell,
> as loud as the rolling thunder.
> The herald strong cried his message well,
> and listening, all down under!
>
> From heaven proclaim I Gehenna's creep:
> From earth has descended a giant!
> He leaps through the dawn 'cross the yawning deep,
> to muffle its weeping affiant.
>
> On elbow raised, each pris'ner sat straight—
> the devils did all resent it.
> They howled like a storm in the darkest night
> and fumed, but could not prevent it!
>
> On elbow raised, each pris'ner sat straight—
> listening as hell never listened.
> They asked about day and they asked about night,
> and feared not the fire that glistened!
>
> On third-day morning, when hell's cock crowed,
> all the ghosts of hell were set flying!
> Bright heavenly sunlight through hell all flowed—
> a dream for both living and dying!
>
> In hell shone bright God's glory and praise,
> gold-coloring deamons and their mates.
> And the walls of hell fell crumbling in the rays,
> off their hinges flew hell's strong gates!"
> (Grundtvig 1944, #243, trans. TH)

But is there any comfort, any good and happy message, for us, who no longer share the conceptions of the Middle Ages (cf. chap. 4, sec. 1), in hearing about a man who in solidarity with those who are murdered by the powerful or who are destroyed by the violence of the system took it upon himself to die, although he did not desire death? Are we not forced to believe that this Jesus was the Son of God, who voluntarily suffered death upon the cross as a substitute for us? Do we not, somehow, by necessity, have to speak of "the joyous exchange," where Jesus takes our misery upon himself and gives us in return his divine righteousness? And if we cannot—because in modernity we can no longer think in terms of the paradox of the incarnation—do we not once more end up with the sad fact that in actuality anyone who sets himself up against injustice and oppression is crushed and destroyed by the powerful? Back then, it took place on a cross, which was the classical, especially Roman way of executing slaves and rebellious elements (cf. Hengel 1977). Today the methods of execution are as a rule quite different, but the result is the same. It ends, now as then, in murder.

But perhaps the problem is posed wrongly—perhaps after many centuries of reading, our dependence upon the theological code is what creates difficulties for us. We would like to interpret the event according to this code, but we can no longer think of a God who lets his son die for the sake of humans. And without this faith in God or in a divine Jesus Christ, we still ask what possible power or force there is in the crucifixion. We cannot find an adequate answer, so we become distressed.

If, however, we let this entire problematic fall, the biblical texts themselves provide another model altogether for our christological reflection. In Paul, the thought appears that Jesus was "the last Adam" or "the second man" (1 Cor. 15:45ff.). Naturally, Paul interprets even this on the basis of the theological code: "the last Adam" is—in contrast to the first—"life-giving," and "the second man" is "from heaven." But if we set this aside, we have here a correlation of the Old Testament's Adam and the New Testament's Jesus, which can also cast light on the crucifixion.

The first human, as described in Genesis 1 and 2, lived in harmony with his cohabitant (Eve), and with surrounding nature. God's spirit was breathed into him, and he did not know force or violence. It is true, of course, that man according to the first creation narrative (Genesis 1) is to rule over nature and over its birds, fish, and four-legged animals, but there is no talk of oppression, much less of extermination. Man is to live from plants that yield seeds and from trees with seeds in their fruit (v. 29). And in the second creation narrative (Genesis 2), birds, fish, and animals are described as Adam's "helpers."

There is no reference to *one* being's oppression of *another.* Adam and Eve are one flesh!

Read against this background, the Second Adam, Jesus, is the man who renounces power and lives without it—and without the violence that follows power like a shadow. For "power" means that one can assert one's own interests, despite the interests of everyone else. This is why there is a need to be on guard against all those who think that power, in one form or another, is a given within the structure of existence (here in Denmark, especially Lögstrup, cf. Glebe-Möller 1982). There is nothing "good" about power. And in the Bible, it is only *after* the fall that Adam must use power (toil) in order to subdue the earth (Gen. 3:17ff.). It is only in the transitory society in which we live that power is inevitable and must be confronted with counterforce: the power of suffering, the force of example. This is the "meaning"—to use Lonergan's phrase—of the doctrine of Christ's second coming: Jesus in principle cancelled all power by dying on the cross, but the final negation of power and violence is still to come.

That Jesus is a human being who without power dies on the cross gives comfort to those who today are broken by the application of power. It gives them hope—in narrative form—that a power-free existence *is* possible. Jesus as the Second Adam is—to use the language of traditional dogmatics—*exemplum*: as he suffered and died, so shall all others suffer and die who counteract the powerful. But he is also—in the same language—*donum* ("gift"): it is his gift to humanity, quite undeserved, that dominance-free existence can be realized in a world full of oppression. This "donum" points beyond life here and now; it points to transcendence—or in the older symbolism, to "God." In the religious experience of spirituality, we experience the ground of being, where peace and not power rules.

But the way to peace—existence without power—is, according to the Bible, via the resurrection. By examining Frye's aforementioned "U-pattern," we see that the resurrection is necessary to the structure of the biblical text. But the fact that it is necessary in the biblical text does not make it necessary in our or the church-community's life, unless we acknowledge the resurrection as the answer to a concrete, political-moral problem in the past—a problem that is still ours today.

The problem, of course, is how we—like the first Christian community—can hold on to the experience: that in the crucifixion, a dominance-free existence is made possible, even though oppression may raise its head again. To this problem there is no theoretical solution, only a practical one. The resurrection is a challenge to our life together: we must, like the first Christian community, share bread and have all things in common (Cf. chap. 2, sec. 7). If we succeed in this, we are on the way *to* peace and *away from* power, on the way to the life of the first Adam in Paradise.

It should be clear enough that according to the interpretation of Jesus' death and resurrection given here, *morality* is an essential element in the church's praxis—yes, the church's praxis is nothing other than morality. The classical distinction of the Reformation, between faith and works, is meaningful only when the death and resurrection of Jesus are interpreted from the theological code. For in that case—and only in that case—the decisive, primary, and foundational element is faith in the death of Christ as salvation for all humans. We are not saying that the Reformers, headed by Luther, did not put emphasis on morality. Of course they did—as we have exemplified in the former chapter. But what was the foundation they could lay for morality? Only the extremely problematic one that "faith bears good fruits." When they were to describe the contents of "the fruits of faith," the Reformers had to distance themselves from "the worldly regiment," because Christianity in their view was incommensurate with this evil world.

But was this not also what Paul claimed in his first letter to the church at Corinth, when he spoke of the contradiction between the world's wisdom and God's? The answer is affirmative, only if "the world" is understood as an ontological contradiction to Christian praxis—and if undergirded by postulates to the theological code concerning the sinfulness of all humans, and so forth. That Paul knows these postulates, and uses them in other contexts, is clear (cf., for example, Rom. 5:12ff.). But in the text we are discussing here (1 Corinthians), "the world" is understood as the ordinary, existing social codes. This is clear from the continuation of Paul's argument:

> For consider your call, brethren; not many of you were wise according to worldly standards, not many were of noble birth; but God chose what is foolish in the world to shame the wise, God chose what is weak in the world to shame the strong, God chose what is low and despised in the world, even things that are not, to bring to nothing things that are, so that no human being might boast in the presence of God. (vv. 26ff.).

Here the contrast between the world and the church is clearly interpreted in social categories. It is the low and despised and weak of this world that God in his wisdom chooses. Otherwise, those in power, the great of this world, could continue to "boast in the presence of God"—that is, to justify their might and greatness to themselves and others. It is in this non-ontological, social sense that there is contradiction between the world's wisdom and the crucifixion, or between the world's wisdom and God's. But here, it is not a differentiation between faith and works, but between the exercise of power and Christian praxis.

3. The Five Universal Rules of Morality

The hands', feet's, and eyes' praxis is of course, when it comes to concretion, distinguishable only by degrees from the talk of "the fruits of the spirit." It follows from the criterion of contextuality in theology or christology that we must take a good look around in our context in order to make this praxis concrete and applicable today. Since our present context is that of modernity, I have in *A Political Dogmatic* pointed to five universal rules that correspond to or can be derived within modernity, and that are founded on the modern idea of a universal communicative fellowship (cf. Glebe-Möller 1987, chap. 3; also Glebe-Möller 1980b, 91ff.). They are the rules against

a) killing,
b) maiming,
c) lying,
d) disrespect for tradition, and
e) causing pain.

I agree with Alasdair MacIntyre when he says that these (or similar) rules have modernity, or more especially its principle of individuation, as their social basis. In reference to the American debate on this subject, between the moral philosophers John Rawls (cf. Rawls 1971, also discussed in Glebe-Möller 1980b, 141ff.) and his antipode Robert Nozick (Nozick 1974, also discussed in Hartnack 1980, 47ff.), MacIntyre writes:

> It is in any case clear that for both Nozick and Rawls a society is composed of individuals, each with his or her own interests, who then have to come together and formulate common rules of life. (MacIntyre 1981, 232)

But if one desires to draw the same conclusion from this feature as MacIntyre does, namely, that all modern moral philosophy is a product of the moral decadence of the modern individualistic industrial society, then in my view one has taken the wrong path. We can try to a certain degree to reconstruct those societies that preceded the industrial society of today, but we cannot go behind the back of modernity. It is simply a fact.[1]

That is why I must also stand in criticism of Stanley Hauerwas's argument that the church, the Christian community, should be able to represent an alternative to *any and all* existing societies—including a society that is formed and informed, as ours is, by modernity. Hauerwas expresses and develops his viewpoint in many different ways, but his thesis is most explicit in the following formulation:

> The church does not exist to provide an ethos for democracy or any other form of social organization, but stands as a political alternative to every nation, witnessing to the kind of social life possible for those that have been formed by the story of Christ. (Hauerwas 1981, 12)

I agree with Hauerwas that the church or the Christian community stands for a distinct political or moral praxis—this should already be clear from our discussion of this in the preceding chapters. I also agree with him when he says that the church's praxis cannot be identical with that of democracy or any other sociopolitical organizational principle. We are prevented from such identification by, to mention only one reason, the metaphysical irony of spirituality (cf. above, chap. 4, sec. 6). But I disagree with Hauerwas when he contrasts the church—halfway ontologically—with *any and all* forms for "world." I must think that there is greater correspondence between the church's praxis and that of democracy than between the Christian community and a dictatorship! If that were not the case, all liberation theology and its interpretation of the Christ-story would be false (as Hauerwas actually comes close to saying, cf. Hauerwas 1981, 233 n. 4). But in this context, I disagree with him especially when he draws direct conclusions from the Christ-story for the church or the church's praxis today. He leaps over the entire question of the process of interpretation which of necessity must develop in the interval between the Christ-story and the modern church's praxis.

This interpretation process once again takes place—as all interpretation does—in an already existing context, one where modernity cannot avoid making a contribution or in which it is itself an essential element. I can illustrate this with one of Hauerwas's own examples. He says, in a discussion of slavery:

> The problem with slavery is not that it violates the "inherent dignity of our humanity," but that as a people we have found that we cannot worship together at the table of the Lord if one claims an ownership over others that only God has the right to claim. (Hauerwas 1981, 106)

Hauerwas is right, of course, when he says that the church's praxis, as we have described it here, cannot permit slavery to exist. But the history of Christianity—from Paul, who commanded slaves to be submissive to their masters (cf. Romans 13 or 1 Cor. 7:20ff.), and Luther, to the slavery of blacks in America—shows that it is actually possible to be a Christian and, at the same time and with the world's best conscience, accept slavery. And again, historically it is modernity—brought to early formulation in the American Declaration of Independence and since then continued in many other human- and civil-rights declarations, and in the democratic social organization itself—that has made the Christian community aware that slavery is incompatible with the church's praxis. In our time, it is the idea of a universal communicative fellowship that in my opinion has contributed most, on the theoretical level, to bringing slavery to discredit—and not the theologians' reflections on the meaning of the last supper.

But what about the peasants of the sixteenth century? Did they not in fact draw the consequences of the idea that the church represents an alternative to every other existing society—in that it speaks to an altogether different type of living than that which is recommended in ordinary social codes—namely, when they claimed that slavery (serfdom) is incompatible with the Christ-story? And one cannot possibly say of them that they were influenced by modernity!

The main difference between them and us, however, is that for them the biblical narratives represented the *only* norm. That is why they had to interpret their own situation in the light of the Bible—and were condemned, as we have seen, by Luther who drew altogether different consequences of the biblical texts. We today can be in sympathy with the peasants' interpretation; we can—on our presuppositions—argue that their interpretation was more correct than that of Luther (and the other Reformers). But we cannot with any sense of propriety claim that the peasants stood "as a political alternative to every nation" and witnessed to another type of social life altogether. They just used the Bible to defend and legitimize the distinct form for social life for which—out of their experience and social horizon—they had to fight: namely, a life style where serfdom did not exist and where "the old rights" (as they said) ruled.

I therefore think that there are solid grounds for claiming that the five rules (assuming they are valid) must play an essential role within the church's praxis today. I shall here attempt, first, to look deeper at the meaning of the fourth rule within a christological and ecclesiastical context. Next, I shall discuss the relationship of suffering to the five rules, and in the process also consider whether the admonition to live in peace represents a contribution to or addition beyond the five rules. Finally, I shall discuss how we must learn to behave according to the five (or perhaps more) rules.

4. Respect for Tradition

Tradition, that which is transmitted, is the collective description for all the codes that a society (or a group within a society) passes on to its new or developing members. No society can endure without such a summation of the codes by whose help the members of the society interpret their own experiences and the society's institutions. Within these codes belong, of course, the religions—yes, until secularization the religions were the most dominant of all widely transmitted codes. But it is now an aspect of modernity, perhaps especially of the phenomenon of individuation, that tradition has gone into dissolution—which is to say, there now exist innumerable traditions in society (Thomas Höjrup has differentiated, in the case of Denmark, between the codes or "life-forms" of the independently wealthy, the workers, the higher functionaries, and the bourgeois, cf. Höjrup 1983, chap. 2). But these life styles, traditions, or codes can again be subdivided, as when one talks about "youth culture," the contrast between town and country, traditional differences between metropolitan areas and provincial cities, and so forth. And in addition comes—on the contemporary, global stage of civilization—the differences between Western traditions and such others as the Asian or African, to which I have already referred. It is this dissolution—or, if one wills, proliferation—of tradition, that makes up at least a significant part of the background for the demand that theology or christology be contextual.

When these many different traditions confront the Christian community, with its praxis, there will be elements within them which Christians clearly must oppose: namely, those codes or subcodes that allow (even require) that some other human beings not be treated as equal conversation partners. *Then* it is imperative to make a clean break, immediately—no compromises possible.

But in many instances we may find it difficult to identify the inequality or oppressiveness of the situation, and therefore effect the separation. Does it, for example, make sense to confront a woman who has lived her whole adult life as her husband's faithful wife and helper, as caretaker of the children and center of the home, saying, you cannot belong to the church, for you have not lived according to Christian praxis—you have accepted oppression? Of course it doesn't! For such a woman may simply have lived according to the (patriarchal) code in which she was brought up and indoctrinated from her childhood, and without subjectively experiencing any oppression. So it is important here, in this first context, that women be accepted and treated as equal participants in the Christian community. This is also a way that the moral demand of respect for tradition is fulfilled.

This demand or rule does not even contradict the New Testament texts that time and again emphasize that to break with the prevailing codes—for example, with the Old Testament's provisions or promises—is at the same time to fulfill them. The Gospel of Luke, for example, has Jesus say, after he has quoted Isa. 61:1ff., "Today this scripture has been fulfilled in your hearing" (Luke 4:21). And in Matthew's Gospel, immediately following the beatitudes of the Sermon on the Mount, he declares, "Think not that I have come to abolish the law and the prophets; I have come not to abolish them but to fulfill them" (Matt. 5:17). This respect for tradition is expressed most clearly in Paul, when he says, "To the Jew I became a Jew, in order to win Jews; to those under the law I became as one under the law—though not being myself under the law—that I might win those under the law. To those outside the law I became as one outside the law—not being without law toward God but under the law of Christ—that I might win those outside the law" (1 Cor. 9:20ff.). Translated into the language of the communicative fellowship, Paul here is saying, although I stand within another tradition than you do, I respect your different traditions in order that there can be honest, equality-based conversation between us. Or as expressed in Grundtvig's well-known lines from *New Year's Morning:*

> Who people will meet
> on level and ground,
> with people must sit
> and make their own sound!
> Who for them will sing,
> must borrow their lingue
> and learn to expire it!
> (Grundtvig 1906, 4: 309; Trans. TH)

But the christology for which I am arguing here is in decisive ways contradictory to the theological code and its ways of interpreting the Jesus-figure (as God's son, who died a predestined death on the cross in order to give us all, oppressed and oppressors, forgiveness of sins). How then is it possible, in ecclesiastical contexts, to fulfill the demand that we respect the tradition? The problem comes to a head most concretely within the space and context of worship, where the theological code dominates ritual and hymn-singing, prayers, and most often also the pastor's sermon. (Theodor Jörgensen, in his review, Jörgensen 1983, 47f., has put some emphasis on this problem; he seems to think that we cannot simultaneously give both modernity and the theological code their due—which of course is correct; but what solution would Jörgensen himself propose for this problem?) There seems to be only one alternative: either, against one's better judgment, to adapt to the theological code, or to break out and organize a new congregation or church. The first would of course be sheer hypocrisy; it would also contradict the fundamental moral rule about speaking the truth. The second would apparently be more consistent—but only apparently:

In the first place, it is quite clearly not correct that the Bible is *only* found on the altar (cf. chap. 2, sec. 9). It is *also* found there. But this means that in actuality it may happen—in fact it always happens—that the interpretation that we have offered here, of the Jesus-figure, and of his followers'—the church's—praxis, is offered and heard there.

In the second place, while the spirituality of the worship service is most often of a passive, purely devotional nature, there is no absolute necessity that it must be so. It can also become or inspire—among other things, by offering a contrast to the one-dimensional, stressed conception of time which characterizes modernity—an active, creative form of spirituality (cf. Glebe-Möller 1987, 77f.).

In the third place, the worship service continues to be the place where the memory of the disciples' or the church's fellowship around the bread is alive—albeit, as a rule, only in a most bloodless and watered-down form: as a stylized and clergy-dominated pilgrimage to the altar.

These are the reasons the alternative cannot be either to adapt to the worship tradition or to discard it *en bloc,* but rather, on the one hand, to respect it precisely for what it is, an essential part of the context in which the story of Jesus lives on and is interpreted anew, and on the other hand, to liberate the subversive elements within the selfsame tradition. Which is to say, to pull them out of their hardened formalism and their ecclesiastical guardianship, and instead reestablish them—perhaps especially the Lord's supper—as concrete manifestations of the congregation's fellowship and solidarity with the suffering. Maybe there are still grounds even for the attempt to revive the old interpretation of the Eucharist as a sacrifice—if by that we mean that Jesus, with his death on the cross, has conquered power and violence (cf. chap. 1, sec. 8).

5. The Meaning of Suffering

Even if reasonable people were able, through dominance-free conversation, to argue their way toward moral rules such as those we have mentioned here (or corresponding ones), it does not immediately follow that they can also find agreement on the need "to take up the cross." But this is what must follow from what we have said here: that the church must go in under suffering, must go the way of the cross. Luther knew this—although, as Bloch caustically remarks (Bloch 1970, 161; 1972, 177), it was for the peasants that he enjoined that "suffering, suffering, cross, cross, that is the Christian law, and not anything else" (Luther 1967, 4:239). The reason for this inconsistency is that although dominance-free conversation or a universal communicative fellowship is the presupposition for everything we say or do in the modern society, it is still not *realized* there. On the contrary, society is, now as before—yes, perhaps even more so now, because of the system's power—an oppressive context. This goes for the Western world as well as for the third world. Congregational praxis is related to the concrete forms that our transitional societies assume. And so it is the suffering of this world that the church is involved in and bent under. There is nothing "positive" in suffering, as there is nothing positive in its underlying cause: power. But suffering is a fact, and if the Christian community is to be in solidarity with the weak and oppressed—otherwise, we have said, it would not be a Christian community—it must take on this suffering, in imitation of the Jesus who is now gone. This, briefly stated, is "the meaning" of the christological hymn in Philippians 2. The introduction of the passage encourages the church to fellowship, love, mercy, and to look "not only to one's own interests, but [also] to the interests of others" (Phil. 2:4; some Greek manuscripts weaken the statement by the word "also," and this is of course also the wording in the authorized Danish translation!). And it continues:

> Have this mind among yourselves, which you have in Christ Jesus, who, though he was in the form of God, did not count equality with God a thing to be grasped, but emptied himself, taking the form of a servant, being born in the likeness of men. And being found in human form he humbled himself and became obedient unto death, even death on a cross. Therefore God has highly exalted him and bestowed on him the name which is above every name, that at the name of Jesus every knee should bow, in heaven and on earth and under the earth, and every tongue confess that Jesus Christ is Lord, to the glory of God the Father. (Phil. 2:5–11)

In *A Political Dogmatic,* I have dismissed this hymn as an expression of "christology from above" (Glebe-Möller 1987, 86). To this, my colleague Theodor Jörgensen has objected "that by this coming of God as man, everything that is otherwise up or down has been turned upside-down" (Jörgensen 1983, 43).[2]

He is right, of course, in suggesting that I have too quickly passed this text by. For as it is normally read in our Danish churches—on Palm Sunday, according to the first lectionary—it serves as a good example of the fact that the subversive elements of the gospel are still preserved within our worship space. I must of course reaffirm that the text represents an incarnation-theology "from above, down," and that it therefore belongs within the theological code, but there is more to say about the text than that.

In his exposition of this text, Peter Kemp emphasizes that according to the exegetical scholars the hymn is older than the interpretations of it that we have from Paul and the Gospel of John (Kemp 1973, 103ff.). It includes a series of symbols—the suffering servant, the Son of man, and so forth—which are found in the Old Testament, and also in Jesus' preaching as described in the Gospels. It thus shows that the myth or "Jesus-poem" itself goes before theological reflection and is the actual basis of faith. I should think that what Peter Kemp and others refer to (in Denmark, for example, Johannes Slök, Slök 1981, is clearly indebted to Kemp) by speaking of mythological or poetic language is a Protestant variant of what Catholics (especially) refer to as spirituality: a dimension, even a linguistic one, that goes further or lies far beyond the power of argumentative reason which we utilize daily in modernity. But the question then is whether this myth, this poem, is an expression of active or passive spirituality. It occurs to me now, on second thought, that read in its context the hymn expresses an active and creative spirituality. The hymn says that Jesus was exalted into lordship *because of* his self-emptying ("*therefore* God has highly exalted him"). The hymn is also set within a frame of exhortations directed to the church: "have this mind among yourselves . . . " (v. 5) and "therefore, my beloved . . . do all things without grumbling or questioning, that you may be blameless and innocent, children of God without blemish in the midst of a crooked and perverse generation, among whom you shine as lights in the world" (v. 12ff.). Brueggemann's interpretation is on target when he writes,

> That tradition of radical criticism is about the self-giving emptiness of Jesus, about dominion through the loss of dominion, and about fullness coming only by self-emptying. The emptying is not to be related to a meditative self-negating, for it is a thoroughly political image concerned with the willing surrender of power; it is the very thing kings cannot do and yet remain kings. Thus the entire royal self-understanding is refuted. The empty one who willingly surrendered power for obedience is the ultimately powerful one who can permit humanness where no other has authority to do so. (Brueggemann 1978, 94)

What Brueggemann understresses, at least in the quotation here, is that that very same humanness—in the form of surrendering power and thereby actively taking upon himself cross and suffering in solidarity with others who are suffering and oppressed—is precisely what the text demands of Christians. The myth or poem in Philippians 2 is a "model" for Christian community praxis—the expression is borrowed from Edward Schillebeeckx, who writes, "This solidarity of Jesus with 'demeaned humanity' . . . Paul makes into a model for the Christians' ethical and religious life" (Schillebeeckx 1977, 167; 1980, 177). In this sense, yes, "everything that is otherwise up or down has been turned upside-down"—that is, viewed in relation to the ordinary codes. And in this same sense, it adds another moral rule to our list: the demand that we actively take upon ourselves other people's suffering.

Closely associated with the demand to suffer is the requirement that the disciples of the church be peacemakers—or more correctly, that they actively fulfill the other side of the same command. In the concrete world, where power dominates, peace is pursued through violence. War, regardless of how it is conducted, is simply a manifestation of violence. To renounce power is therefore also to give up the right to wage war or to do wartime service. And to renounce the right to wage war is to make peace.

This is why the Bible speaks so much about peace. When the theological code takes over the interpretation of the requirement of peacemaking, however, it takes on a note of passive, nonobligatory spirituality, as for example in this verse by Grundtvig:

> Peace that soothes our bitter pain
> God us gave in Jesus' name,
> peace he bought us with his blood—
> peace as Jesus with us stood.
> Christendom is in a sum
> *pax* and *evangelium*.
> (Den danske Salmebog, *The Danish Hymnal,* #389, Trans. TH)

That there exists such a religious correlation of experience, of "peace in Jesus" and through Jesus peace with the very ground of being, is undeniable. Nor can we deny that peace understood in this manner can be obtained in the space of worship, and especially through participation in holy communion. It is possible that it is this form for peace that Paul also wishes his colaborers and their congregations, when as a rule he opens his letters with formulas like "Grace to you and peace from God the Father and the Lord Jesus Christ" (Phil. 1:2).

But in the Gospels, it is not this form for peace that is spoken of. "Blessed are the peacemakers, for they shall be called the sons of God" (Matt. 5:9) is a demand put upon the Christian community, a demand for praxis: that it should work actively to overcome conflicts and accomplish reconciliation between people. If this command is heeded, the church is following Jesus, and as he became the son of God, the church's members also become God's children.

That the command to be peacemakers is also a command to be willing to take up suffering is clear from the immediate continuation of Matthew's Gospel: "Blessed are those who are persecuted for righteousness' sake, for theirs is the kingdom of heaven. Blessed are you when men revile you and persecute you and utter all kinds of evil against you falsely on my account" (Matt. 5:10f.). Those who make peace are persecuted, for the powerful do not desire peace. This is clear a little later in the chapter, in the command to love the enemy:

> You have heard that it was said, "You shall love your neighbor and hate the enemy." But I say to you, Love your enemies and pray for those who persecute you, so that you may be sons of your Father who is in heaven. (v. 43f.)

To love the enemy or the persecutor does not of course mean that in some psychologically impossible way one must nurture loving feelings toward one's oppressors. Even the verb "love" refers to praxis. The New Testament's "agape" is not passive—as Martin Luther King, Jr., also emphasized (cf. Glebe-Möller 1980b, 51). On the one hand, it is a matter of not pitching violence against violence or new oppressiveness against old oppression. On the other hand, this means that one unveils, through active nonviolence and the suffering that this inevitably leads to, that it is the enemy or the oppressor who himself is imprisoned in the system of oppression. One gives him the opportunity to see himself as the one who breaks the moral rules. Only when this does not succeed—and how could it possibly be successful, for example, against a South American or Asian military dictatorship?—can the command to love the enemy lead to the abandonment of nonviolent strategies or to situations where the work for peace must be continued, if necessary, with violent means. For in that case the oppressor must be convinced of his breach of the moral rules by the preparedness of the oppressed to position themselves for resistance. This is the fundamentally correct core of the old doctrine of "the just war." But the point is that only those who suffer oppression have the right to decide when to give up nonviolence and proceed to active resistance. This is so, both morally and epistemologically.

Only those whose life-context or "horizon" is marked by violence and oppression and persecution can identify violence and draw its limits. Those in whose life-context violence plays no role, stand outside and cannot speak meaningfully of violence or oppression. Not even in the moral sense can another decide when the persecuted or oppressed shall take a stand for resistance. That would contradict the demand or rule of acknowledging another as an equal conversation partner. At the most, perhaps, one can have an opinion as to when the time has come to discard the strategy of nonviolence, and then through discussions and negotiations attempt to reach agreement about it with the oppressed—but still the risk is that one's argument will be rejected.

When some groups within gnostic Christianity rejected martyrdom (cf. above, chap. 5, sec. 2), they were thus in principle correct. For just as nobody else can decide when I am to offer resistance, so nobody else—in this case, the bishops of the early church—can decree how long the nonviolence strategy is to continue. That can only be decided in the fellowship of the Christian community. In contrast, Luther clearly sinned—both morally and epistemologically—when, on the one hand, he lectured the peasants about their Christian duty and condemned their rebellion, and on the other hand, encouraged the rulers to beat them down as mad dogs! For the peasants' situation was not his. He had therefore no moral right to decide on their behalf whether the limit was reached or not (to avoid misunderstanding: I do not here—or in chap. 6, above—criticize Luther personally; I only criticize the conclusions that are generally drawn from reading the Jesus-narratives from the standpoint of the theological code, as exemplified by Luther).

But is it not, nevertheless, a breach of the church's peacemaking praxis to offer resistance? Must we not, then, draw the conclusion that humans are never as good—or as Christian—as they should be? Against an argumentation of this kind it is worthwhile to offer the reminder that *the actant Jesus,* according to the narratives of the New Testament, always called forth conflict and sowed dissension. Programmatically, Matthew's Gospel states:

> Do not think that I have come to bring peace on earth; I have not come to bring peace, but a sword. For I have come to set a man against his father, and a daughter against her mother, and a daughter-in-law against her mother-in-law; and a man's foes will be those of his own household. (Matt. 10:34–36)

The contrast peace/sword sets the limits for how spiritually "transposed" this text can be interpreted. It is not a question of metaphors here. Naturally, in the perspective of the theological code, it would lie close to understanding the sword as "the world's resistance to Jesus' message of salvation." A consequence would then be the affirmation of the martyr ideology. But in actuality, the text says that *Jesus* "brings" the sword. Jesus is the subject. And this means that *the praxis* that he has left behind among his disciples, in the church community, is a praxis that again and again leads to violent conflicts, namely, when the Christian community, which stakes everything on brotherhood, sisterhood, and fellowship, must defend itself against those in power who only want oppression, because oppression is the only way in which they can retain their status.

So, when in the current peace debate it is said that "peace is the cause above all causes" (Ole Jensen), this is not correct in the light of the church's praxis. If peace is simply the peaceful acceptance of oppressive rulers, it is worth nothing—or rather: the sword is preferable, because only through conflict and the sword can the oppressed obtain their rights. Luther obviously was sidetracked in this matter. For although he defended peace and condemned war for the sake of the weak and poor (as emphasized by Per Frostin, Frostin 1983, 95ff.), he was neither—like many contemporary spokesmen for peace. But what could he then say on their behalf?

The background for claiming that peace is the cause above all causes is of course the contemporary nuclear arms race and the global threat it represents. War has now assumed a "metaphysical" dimension, as Ole Jensen says, (cf. Jensen 1983, 43), for now it is the whole planet, the home of all humans and animals, that is threatened. The question arises, however, whether this metaphysical (or perhaps better: cosmological) expansion of war, or threat of war, in reality makes peace the cause above all causes. For if violence and oppression accelerate in the world, in all possible variations from open and explicit physical repression to the more hidden and streamlined violence of the system —and if at a given point in time nothing is left but sheer physical life, on the one hand, and violence and oppression on the other—well, then it is conceivable that war, atomic war, might be the worthiest or best *finale* to humankind's history. Humans, after all, do not live by bread alone. Without morality and humanity, physical life is worth nothing. That was something the peasants in the sixteenth century understood. It was not their existence that was at stake—on the whole, in fact, some scholars think they were relatively well heeled. But the lords and masters took away their humanity, their human worth. And so they had to create an uprising, put up resistance, start a war.

The conclusion, then, is: of course, the Christian must work for peace. Surely the Christian community must be a peacemaking one. And in all circumstances, the enemy must be loved. But the demand that we shall make peace is not an absolute demand, for it cannot without qualifications—as I have tried to indicate here—be put before the interests of the weak, the oppressed, the persecuted. The only demand that is absolute is the demand that we be ready to take up suffering. This is so, regardless of whether we are fighting for the cause of peace by way of nonviolence or instead decide to put up resistance against the oppressor. "Suffering, suffering, cross, cross, that is the Christian law," said Luther. And in this sense he was principally correct! Our passage from Matthew's report of Jesus' charge to his disciples continues:

> He who loves father or mother more than me is not worthy of me; and he who loves son or daughter more than me is not worthy of me; and he who does not take his cross and follow me is not worthy of me. He who finds his life will lose it, and he who loses his life for my sake will find it. (Matt. 10:37–39)

To work for peace simply for peace' sake cannot be the church's praxis if we are to stand in the succession of Jesus. Such a praxis is unworthy of him. Worthy only is that praxis that defends peace by taking up the cross. But that praxis is not something one simply falls—or jumps—into the first time one is confronted with the figure of Jesus. It is something that takes exercise, training, learning—just as do all other dimensions of Christian praxis.

6. Training in Christianity

The expression "training in Christianity" is, as many will know, taken from Sören Kierkegaard (it is the title of his pseudonymous work from 1850 ascribed to Anti-Climacus, cf. Kierkegaard 1963)—although I am not relying on his thoughts on the subject here.[3]

In our context here, the phrase simply says that to be a Christian—to participate in the church community's praxis—takes training and instruction. Luther claimed that prayer, meditation, and "trial" (*tentatio*) make a right Christian. But even prayer and meditation—two forms of spirituality—must, as we have seen (cf. chap. 3, sec. 6), be exercised. And "trial," which we can translate here as rejection of the temptation to submit to ordinary or prevailing codes or of the temptation to use power (cf. above, concerning the temptations of Jesus), also takes practice. A temptation becomes a "trial" when it corresponds to the dominant social codes, where the use of power is the essential ingredient. If one is to conquer that temptation, one must train oneself in being a peacemaker and must learn a different code, namely, the church's or Jesus'.

The thought that Christianity requires training is an old one. It was alive in Catholic Christianity throughout the Middle Ages (and is still alive in part today). Back then, it had close ties to the doctrine of virtues, namely, the four Aristotelian "cardinal virtues": justice, prudence, temperance, and courage; and the three Pauline ones: faith, hope, and love. Within the concept of virtue (*virtus*) lies the thought that moral life—in this case Christian moral life—consists in training oneself, practicing, to be able to act justly, exhibit prudence, show temperance, courage, love, and other qualities. One who constantly trains and exercises and thus develops the ability to act justly, to exhibit prudence, and so on, is a virtuous man or woman. And we are all, according to medieval thought, called by Christ to be virtuous people.

In modern times the doctrine of virtues has receded into the background—our modern moral thought centers more on the communicative fellowship and the universal moral rules that, for reasons I have indicated above, have emerged in modernity (cf. also Glebe-Möller 1980b). But there are good reasons to bring it to the forefront again today, even though we cannot in every detail take on an Aristotelian or Thomistic moral philosophy. In the context of christology, the doctrine of virtues is useful in pointing out that the stories of Jesus are not only for intellectual gratification or private edification (even though they may be that too!), but are first and foremost put before us as models for the Christian community's conduct. That is the case when we think of those actions which the actant in the texts carries out, and it goes for the entire enterprise which the writing of the texts represented:

> Now Jesus did many other signs in the presence of the disciples, which are not written in this book; but these are written that you may believe that Jesus is the Christ, the Son of God, and that believing you may have life in his name. (John 20:30)

This passage can of course also be interpreted according to the theological code—that is perhaps how John himself takes it. But if we interpret "believing" as the eyes' praxis (cf. chap. 2, sec. 4), as a clear break with the prevailing social codes and the reading of Jesus as the one who brings salvation for life and body—and if we understand "the Son of God," as Sobrino does, as a designation for Jesus' own praxis—then this passage will be seen to say that the Gospel of John was written in order to provide the church a model for its praxis after Jesus' death.

But in order to be a virtuous Christian person, it is not enough that one trains oneself, practices, and exercises the seven virtues willy-nilly. There must be wholeness and consistency in the virtuous person's life and actions. The virtuous person must—in Stanley Hauerwas's expression—be a *character*. And character is something the members of the Christian community develop when they allow *their* actions to parallel those in the narratives concerning Jesus' activities. Christian character—or identity, to use another expression (cf. above, chap. 6, sec. 1)—is only present when the stories of Jesus "affect" us, or when the members of the Christian community become the children of God, just as he became the Son of God. This kind of identity is not a gift, however—something one receives suddenly and undeservedly. It requires hard work and training, even intellectually —Aristotle rightly counted *phronesis* (approximate translation, "moral intelligence") as one of the central virtues (cf. MacIntyre 1981, 144f.). That is why the New Testament letters are literally swarming with exhortations and instructions for the churches. They often strike us as tiresome and irritating in all their timebound moralism. But here and there they can be quite precise and relevant—as for example when the Letter to the Hebrews refers the Christian community to the "faith" that Jesus, "the pioneer of faith," practiced:

> Let us run with perseverance the race that is set before us, looking to Jesus the pioneer and perfecter of our faith, who for the joy that was set before him endured the cross, despising the shame, and is seated at the right hand of the throne of God. Consider him who endured from sinners such hostility against himself, so that you may not grow weary or fainthearted. (Heb. 12:1–3; cf. Glebe-Möller 1987, 90)

But as we have said several times, the Jesus-story does not live exclusively in the church or within the space of worship. Christian character or identity can be practiced and exercised in altogether different places, even by people who do not perceive of themselves as Christian. In the following—and last—chapter, I shall discuss whether Christian identity can be present in the new religiosity of today.

Notes

1. Theodor Jörgensen, in his review of *A Political Dogmatic* (Jörgensen 1983, 35f.), cannot determine how I relate to modernity. As I see it, modernity is simply a fact just like the weather! There are aspects of modernity that undoubtedly must be fought—for example, the effects of individuation—but even individuation is a fact. There are finally also, morally speaking, positive aspects of modernity. Individuation does not only mean isolation and atomization, but also

autonomy: that human beings are enabled to assume moral responsibilities of which they would not—for example in the tribal society or in the agrarian extended family—even have been able to perceive. Certainly, in this context one must say, as MacIntyre's thesis goes, that morality understood as individual responsibility over against universal moral laws is again a modern phenomenon. But the consequence of such reflections is simply a confirmation of the fact that when we think morally today, we cannot do so independently of modernity.

2. Jörgensen also charges that I have not respected the differences between my different sources—Pannenberg, Moltmann, Schillebeeckx and Sobrino—and have shown no interest in the fact that my *reasoning* (Jörgensen's italics) is not shared by those theologians I have referred to as also rejecting "the christology from above." Relative to the first point, Jörgensen is quite right—though I indicated a shared *tendency* only. But with regard to the second point, I do not think he is right. The four theologians mentioned are all, in my judgment, engaged with "my" problem: the problem of modernity. Only the approach is different, and they are all, if compared with me, much too dependent on the theological code. Cf. also, however, my references to Schillebeeckx, below.

3. The reason I do not follow Kierkegaard here is first and foremost that even though this particular book of his stresses the need to follow and imitate the descended Christ, he is deeply dependent on the theological code. Moreover, he defines his project in relation to surroundings which at least pro forma are understood as Christian ("the established Christendom" in Kierkegaard's expression). This situation no longer exists in the era of secularization. So if Kierkegaard's thoughts are to be utilized today, they must be reinterpreted—and that is a project that goes beyond my powers. In Denmark, this has been started by Kresten Nordentoft (1973).

8. Neo-Religiosity and the Jesus Story

1. Religious Worldviews and the Jesus Story

In *A Political Dogmatic,* and in the preceding chapters here, I have started from the assumption that secularization is a fact that cannot be explained away. We are therefore forced—as Bonhoeffer already was aware (speaking of a "non-religious interpretation of biblical concepts," cf. Bonhoeffer 1966, 233; 1972, 285ff.)—to ask about the validity of the Jesus story in a modern world where people no longer think or talk about God and where the language of the theological code has lost its grip. But is this a correct starting point? Do we not see everywhere around us a new awakening of religious interest—even here in the Western world (cf. Jörgensen 1983, 38f.)? Does the phenomenon we describe in general terms as "neo-religiosity" not represent the best counter-proof to the secularization thesis?

That there exist religious events and experiences, now as before, we have no reason to doubt. Spirituality, especially passive spirituality, is a possibility also for modern people. Moreover, neo-religious movements (or better: youth religions) often carry with them ideas and impulses from the higher religions, including Christianity. Even outside the youth religions, among Western youth generally, one often encounters attempts to say in a modern language something of what Christianity at one time could say. Steven Spielberg's film *E.T.* has an appeal for millions and millions of young people in the Western world. In the film, E.T., a curious little being from another planet, appears in a number of situations that Jesus was also faced with, according to the New Testament. Think only of E.T.'s descent from the spaceship—a modern appendix to the christological hymn in Philippians 2. Or of E.T.'s death, revivification, and departure in the spaceship—step by step repeating the resurrection and ascension motifs in modern garb. But the new religious interests apparent in the Western world are clearly different, and on decisive points, from the Jesus-narratives of the Gospels and the Christian community's praxis, as I have interpreted them here. And the social impact of youth religions does not in any way correspond to traditional roles of Christianity or of other higher religions.

I shall first sketch the religious situation in the Western world by reference to concepts drawn from Jürgen Habermas. In his latest and largest work, *Theory of Communicative Action,* he speaks of "the linguistification of the sacral." By this he means "the transposition of cultural reproduction, social integration, and socialization from the foundations of the sacrality to linguistic communication and consensus-oriented action" (Habermas 1981, 2:163; 1987, 2:97). The thesis he is arguing in this work, with support from Max Weber and Emile Durkheim in particular, is, namely, that in modernity culture, society, and personality is not built on the foundations of religious or sacral traditions, but on consensus in language and mutual understanding. It is through linguistic communication that we develop a culture, organize a society, and develop ourselves into personalities or persons. *Before* modernity, wherever we place its beginnings, our existence was built on tradition, and the tradition was encamped in a worldview that was religious. This means, in the first instance, that the worldview simply was not up for debate. Culture, society, personality—they were all formed in correspondence with the norms that were established in or by this worldview.

If we look closer at the pre-modern worldview, we find that it contained the notion of a divine power, principally independent of the profane world, to which humans were responsible and whose function or task was to assure everyone that the unequal distribution of happiness in the world would finally be corrected, here or beyond. This corresponds to Max Weber's idea that all the great historical religions arose as answers to the problem of theodicy (Habermas 1981, 1:280; 1984, 1:201). But in modernity, this notion does not exist any longer. This means that the problem of theodicy demands a new, "linguistic" solution: we are condemned to give *reasons*—whether reactionary or progressive, conservative or socialist—for the fact that the world's goods are distributed unequally. Much has been lost in this erosion of tradition—we all, in fact, suffer under it—but to Habermas's way of thinking, what we are up against is an irreversible process that can only be halted or slowed down temporarily by regressions.

In other words, it is Habermas's thesis that *secularization* is an unavoidable feature in the modern worldview, and that this world picture, moreover, is not a singular one. The picture of the world in the modern period has been "de-centered," he says, in the many pictures of the "objective," the "social," and the "subjective" *worlds*. In relation to the first, the objective world, we speak in terms of true (or false) sentences. It is the world of the natural sciences, modern physics, and technology. In relation to the second, the social world, we speak in terms of right (or wrong) sentences. It is the economic-political-moral world. And finally, in relation to the subjective world, the world of personality, we speak in sentences that are truthful (or untruthful).

Even though certain religious experiences continue to exist, it seems clear to this way of thinking that the *religious picture of the world* no longer exists. This has the immediate consequence that religion—in the Western, primarily the Christian, world—becomes more and more politicized. We see this even in the Danish folk church, for example, while the theological code continues to dominate, one finds among younger priests and church members a growing political involvement. This manifests itself among other ways in an increasing involvement in ecological issues, and in the fact that relatively large numbers of young Christians, both in Denmark and in the rest of the Western world, are joining the peace movement (cf. the prev. chap.).

Not even the neo-religious movements, which reject this kind of politicization, consider themselves confronted with transcendent and binding worldviews. Moreover, they make their appeal only to a very narrowly limited sector of the population: socially and religiously interested youth from the middle classes between the ages of fifteen and twenty-five (cf. Haack 1981, 29, 58ff., 77). How many people are involved is difficult to say with precision. From the few empirical data that are available, it would seem that only a few decimals of one percent of the present youth generation have joined one (or more!) of these movements. And because of this the youth religions are already clearly different from the higher religions—in our case Christianity—whose world picture, until the breakthrough of capitalism or industrialization in the last century, was the normative basis for all the members of society, regardless of class, age, or gender.[1]

2. Characteristics of Youth Religions

The existing classifications of the youth religions are not very useful, since on the whole they all take their starting point in the higher religions—which the youth religions, according to the preceding material, have very little to do with. We are not thereby saying that they do not pick up elements from the higher religions. On the contrary, it seems to be the case that they are all heavily syncretistic. For example, within "Subud," which is usually classified as an Islamic-inspired movement, one operates with references to both Mohammed and Jesus (these represent the male and female principles, respectively). One can hardly expect anything else. When the classical higher religions no longer provide authoritative and binding world images for a given culture or a given society, the new religions that emerge among the youth will naturally assume features that have their roots in the otherwise mostly eroded traditions of the culture or society in which they emerge. An important common feature for most of the youth religions seems to be the Eastern (or Indian) inspiration. But one must here be aware that this inspiration in most cases has been mediated via the U.S.A. Much as the case was with the youth revolt, the student uprising, the hippie culture, and so on, the principal geographical point of origin seems to have been California. This is undoubtedly associated with the fact that the American west coast is the place where the Asian influence is first felt—among other things, because of Asian immigrants. Once they are established on American soil, however, these movements are quickly taken over by American commercialization and, as part of the ordinary influence of American culture in the West, they soon spread to Europe and assume all the characteristics of multinational corporations.

This "Americanization" can naturally also go hand in hand with fanatical anticommunism—as in the case of the "Unification church," whose founder Sun Myung Moon hails from South Korea, and which is reportedly heavily infiltrated by the South Korean intelligence system. American anticommunism has its origin in the reaction to the October Revolution, and is to a degree understandable, since the U.S.S.R. by definition is the contradiction of the liberal and capitalist social system in the U.S.A. It is therefore reasonable to assume that the youth religions will flourish in the Western world as long as American capitalism is able to keep its dominant position, and for as long as the overt and covert confrontation between the superpowers U.S.A. and U.S.S.R. goes on. And the fact that these young people, once they have become attracted to youth religions, go on pilgrimages to India and other Eastern cultures is in and of itself not such a strange thing at all. Nor even that some of them, after their visit to India, return home and organize a new religion such as for example "Janakananda," which has obtained a not inconsiderable following in Scandinavia.

Otherwise, the American influence also makes itself felt in those parts of the neo-religious movements that are explicitly associated with Christian traditions. It was for example first and foremost the meeting with the American Jesus-movement that gave the Danish Jesus-groups ("Young Christians" and others) their earliest nudge (cf. Værge 1974 and n.d.).

If we look a little deeper into the social structure of the youth religions, it seems to contain three characteristic features: "the holy master," "the saving prescription," and "the saved family" (the following is based on Haack 1981, 30ff.). The holy master is a leader-figure who with unlimited authority stands at the head of each youth religion. It is this leader who has the saving prescription, and it is the leader who will realize salvation and solve (almost) all the problems of humanity. He must therefore be honored by his followers, among other things by special names of honor. The holy master's position and leadership role is emphasized in the teachings of the youth religions themselves. The leader of "The Children of God," Moses David (previously David Berg), says for example:

> The leader is not always right, but he is the leader. Here God shows us that although the leader does something you believe to be wrong or unbiblical, you must rather avoid making objections, for God determined him to be the leader. (Haack 1981, 32)

To obey the holy master (or those of his adjutants who derive their authority from him) will first and foremost mean that one follows those rules and principles that he has established concerning his disciples' life and conduct: the saving prescription. For example, the followers of "Ananda Marga" are required to walk the road to redemption, "Sadhana." The road is described in sixteen points that can be excerpted as follows (several of the points, apparently, only apply to the male members of the movement!):

1. washing in cold water after urinating
2. keeping the foreskin clean
3. letting all body hair grow
4. wearing tight underwear and loose-fitting outer garments
5. washing the body before meditation, meals, and so forth
6. taking daily cold showers in a sitting position
7. controlling food intake
8. fasting on certain days
9. meditating twice daily
10. having the goals embodied by the guru always before one's eyes

11. always following the ideology of self-liberation and service to mankind
12. following the rules of conduct (certain body motions, and so forth)

and if one lives according to this "saving prescription," one achieves "the white peace"!

Finally, "the saved family" is the designation for the group of followers or devotees that the new disciple first meets (he or she has little if any direct contact with the holy master). The saved family consists of older and newer followers. It exhibits typical self-assurance and is outwardly strongly goal-oriented. This, naturally, makes a great impression on newcomers. And if he or she should separate from the saved family, salvation is lost outright. If one is expelled, one has nothing to hold on to. That is why young people who at one point may have broken ties with such groups nevertheless often return. "Inside" there is order and salvation. "Outside" there is chaos and destruction.

The three features mentioned here may of course exhibit several points of similarity with the first Christian movement, the early "Jesus movement" (Gerd Theissen's term, Theissen 1979, chap. 1), but the differences are also quite apparent. I shall mention only three. First, Jesus demands that his disciples become followers, not cadavers. Second, Christian praxis is not centered on the development of the individual personalities within the community's membership, but on solidarity with the suffering and the oppressed. And finally, it is not the participation in the community of faith that is the presupposition for salvation; "salvation"—to refer to it by that classical concept—consists in showing through praxis that one belongs to the community.

3. Youth Religions and Their Social Causes

In *The Sacred Canopy,* Peter L. Berger has pointed out that with secularization, the original religious "canopy"—roughly corresponding to what with Habermas I have here called the religious world picture—has definitively broken down and been exchanged for a long series of religious appeals, each of which seems attractive to specific groups of people (Berger 1967, 105–53). Berger's description is built on the American situation in the first half of the sixties, but it is today clearly relevant also on the Danish (or on the whole Western) scene. The phenomenon he describes is also referred to by the rather vague designation "pluralism."

The youth religions as such are clearly expressions of pluralism. Each and every one of them offers, in competition with the others and with all the rest of the original religious traditions that are institutionalized in the churches, a definition of reality and a pattern for living one's life. The competitive situation demands capital and a program of marketing, and this naturally involves the necessity of a bureaucracy—this is especially evident in "Scientology," the "Unification church," and "TM." The youth religions have as their target audience the youth of the Western world (although some, for example, "Divine Light Mission," are also operative in India). The question is: why do portions of youth population "buy into" this appeal?

One factor is the general influence of American culture which I have already mentioned. This has affected not just the young people, but the general populations in all Western countries. But here we must acknowledge that the young people especially—those who have grown up since World War II, in contrast to the older generation—have not known any other culture. At least not city youths. "Urbanization" is an important factor also, since it was in the big cities that the traditional world pictures were first and most devastatingly broken up. This also is connected with the fact that the traditional worldviews had their basis in agricultural society (cf. Glebe-Möller 1987, chap. 2).

Another factor, probably amplified by the economic crisis in the Western world, is the increased attraction to the irrational. For many, especially for young people, the instrumental or functional rationality of Western industrial societies seems to have played into bankruptcy: ecological problems and the threat of nuclear obliteration are the most visible symptoms. In this situation, such as it appears to most of us in the Western world, a turn to some form of spirituality—in the broadest sense—appears to be the only solution. Even the so-called charismatic movements can be understood against this background, although in Catholic contexts, they of course have longer spiritual traditions to draw on, and in Protestant circles incorporate certain older, so-called free church impulses. One can mention, for instance, the Quakers, who originally sprang from Puritan Calvinism but now allow the leading of the Spirit to be the only principle of guidance for their "silent meetings." In Denmark, one of the reasons for the popularity of K. E. Lögstrup's authorship is undoubtedly that people here, in Lögstrup's metaphysical view of the cosmos, find inspiration for the confrontation with the ecological crisis (cf. Ole Jensen 1983, 43f.).

The ecological threat, together with the threat of nuclear annihilation, places many young people in an apocalyptic mood that can be a parallel to what the early Christians, or Luther and the other Reformers, lived with. And here, religious phenomena prove to have a "mobilizing function," because religion—as Danièle Léger has shown in an investigation of French agricultural collectives—"appears to be in discontinuity with the ruling culture, since it does not [not any longer] seem allied with the thoughtforms that lie at the center of the logic of catastrophe which they [the young] condemn" (Léger 1982, 60). So the struggle of the agricultural collectives to cultivate the soil in ways that are ecologically correct, thus contrasting it to the surrounding industrially polluted soil, can be correspondingly interpreted by the young on the basis of the religious difference between the sacral and the profane—with the young, of course, themselves inhabiting the sacral space.

But when it is proven, according to the information available, that it is especially those between eighteen and twenty-five years of age—and from the middle layers of society—that allow themselves to be affected by youth religions, the reasons we have mentioned cannot be decisive. One must assume that what has been called the "prolonged puberty" also plays a role. We mean by this the fact that a very large percentage of youth are not, as earlier, sent out on the labor market ("out to work") after a brief period of schooling (or none at all). While the youth of earlier eras were considered "grownups"—that is, had to assume the tasks and obligations of adults by confirmation (cf. the classical phrase from confirmation addresses, "today you enter the ranks of adults")—they, especially the middle-class young, are now held in a sort of no-man's-land from the time they are about fourteen until they have finished some form of education. On the one hand, they constitute a group by themselves ("youth in school"), but on the other hand they are really not counted, because they do not actually find themselves in the adult world.

This situation is impacted by two characteristic features in the social psychology of Western youth: one is the breakdown of parental authority, the other—and correspondingly—is narcissism. On the first point, modern scholars write:

> The generation of parents has no socially adequate qualifications to make them stand out as obvious models for identification. Their own socialization has taken place under substantially different social conditions, and their vocational and cultural qualifications are already out-dated, so to speak. They are already, in any number of areas, overtaken by the young who often know more about the society into which they are to grow than their parents do. (Illeris et al. 1982, 100)

On the other point, it is sufficient here only to say that narcissism is a natural consequence whereby parents disappear as identification objects. We are not simply talking about self-centeredness in the common, everyday sense of the term—though also about that!—but rather about a situation in which a young person no longer finds anything to hold on to within the family, and especially not in the parents, and therefore must try to find something within him- or herself, or alternatively, in groups of people of the same age and the same mind ("group narcissism").

In a way, the young of the middle class are the most vulnerable. They are the ones who attend colleges and universities, and who to an extraordinary degree are being pressured between parental ambitions and social qualification requirements, on the one hand, and their lack of identification-possibilities and consequent narcissism, on the other. The present situation among high school and college students generally can be described as follows:

> There are different demands and norms in the home, in the school, among friends, and eventually also at work. There is the eternal conflict and bad conscience related to class requirements and homework. There is the conflict between cooperation and competition. There is falling in love and sexuality, which comes at cross-purposes with everything else. There is the daily bombardment of knowledge one must obtain, opinions and problems one must come to terms with. There is the pressure from the outer world with its meaningless wars, arms race, atomic power, and waste of resources. There is philosophy, Almighty God, and Marx. (Illeris et al. 1982, 141)

It does not take much imagination to see that such young people—especially when they are sharp enough to see that something is wrong (cf. Haack 1981, 29, 58ff., 77)—must be an easy target for the youth religions. Here they are confronted with an absolute authority that replaces the parents ("the holy master"). Here they get an irrational explanation of (an irrational) reality, and a set of rules for living that do not contradict narcissism—on the contrary. As authoritative as the rules of "Ananda Marga" are, they appeal equally to self-observation and self-reflection. And in the "saved family," they have their group narcissism satisfied. No wonder that the youth religions have consciously sought to infiltrate the educational sphere (Haack 1981, 419ff.).

This does not mean that the best known and most widespread youth religions of today will continue to grow through the eighties and nineties. "The Children of God," "Divine Light Mission," and the "Ananda Marga" movements, for example, have all lost much of their edge in the last few years. In Denmark, the charismatic movement has clearly outstripped the Jesus-movement of the sixties. But other movements of more or less similar character continue to emerge. I shall close by looking at some that quite fittingly could be called "body religions"!

4. The New Body Religions

If one visits any large Western European or North American bookstore these days, one will find a section devoted to books entitled *The Massage Book, Body Consciousness, Handbook of Zone Therapy, The Ways of the Body,* among others. In the last few years, a huge market has apparently developed here, which has—at least tangentially—connections with the youth religions that we have discussed in the previous section. The new body religions have their own characteristic features.

The youth religions can be described as religions because they contain—at least to a degree—strongly syncretistic elements of the world pictures of the higher religions. In these movements, the most typical point is to attach oneself to a certain master's teaching and then to seek to follow these prescriptions in more or less closed groups. And, as we have said, the target audience is the young of the middle class, those around twenty years of age.

In the phenomenon that I am attempting to describe here, the doctrinal aspects are secondary (although they are naturally there—and not less syncretistic than in the youth religions). The group-dimension (the concept of the saved family) also plays a subordinate role. It is typical for the body religions that the preferred "initiation" process is a weekend seminar that is offered for—and open to—everyone. Just call this number! When the seminar is full, the telephone will not be answered! As for the target audience, the appeal seems to be aimed at "the yuppies"—relatively highly educated, middle and upper-middle class persons between twenty-five and forty-five years old.

The key phrase in this market is *body consciousness.* The point of entry is presented in *The Ways of the Body* as follows:

> The body is a medium. It is the channel through which you as an individual can express yourself and live on this earth. Reduction of its life limits your possibilities for fulfilling contact with other human beings, with nature, and with the outer world as a whole. The recovery of the body is the designation for the conscious effort to explore the interaction of spirit and body,

> between thought, feelings, will, and movement. There is no way to a living body. It *is* the way. (Sathyarthi 1982, 1, 13)

There are clearly religious over- or undertones in this passage. Jesus, as we know, said, "I am the way, the truth and the life," and other religious founders have said the same. Here, it is the body that is the way. Actually, the body religions often refer to the god-concept in their musings. "Look not for God in heaven. Look for God in your own body," says Bhagwan Shree Rajnesh, another of the gurus of the youth religions. The emphasis is on self-therapy: if one knows one's own body—that is, as it functions in concert with nature and the universe—one can partly avoid, partly cure all illnesses and hurts that otherwise plague humans in the Western industrialized world (in spite of the Eastern-inspired tone, the "message" is obviously directed to the Western world). In these various therapies and introductions to body consciousness, one is totally oblivious to the sociological or sociologically-based reasons for human misery. The therapies are therefore individualistic in the extreme—as is clear from the choice of words in the above passage ("through which you as an individual can express yourself"). A therapy in the form of "healing," discussed below, presupposes of course that there is one who heals and one (or more) who is healed. But here it is *I* who am healed—yes, we are even presented, paradoxically, with certain techniques for "self-healing"! Social structures do not enter the picture at all. The individualistic and cosmological character of the movement is clearly expressed in the press-release for *The Ways of the Body,* where the caption reads: "Your body is the part of the universe that is closest to you!"

If we think, in contrast, of classical Christianity or Judaism, we shall find that *here* the command to love of neighbor has been put at the core of religion. The body religions, on the other hand, clearly express an attitude that—according to Christopher Lasch—characterizes the whole of Western industrial culture: narcissism (Lasch 1979).

If we should try to conceptualize some social conditions or sociological reasons for the flourishing of the body religions, it would fall close-to-hand to refer to the stress of modern living. Stress is of course itself only a symptom for the deeper maladies in industrial society, perhaps above all in the large cities. I have tried to identify some of these maladies in the chapter on "Modernity" in *A Political Dogmatic* (cf. Glebe-Möller 1987, chap. 1; also above, chap. 4, sec. 1). Most important in our context is perhaps "futurity." This, briefly stated, refers to the fact that the inhabitants of the modern metropolis are always, on the one hand, busy, and are never, on the other hand, able to rest (cf. Kiselberg et al. 1982, secs. 13–14). The psychosomatic consequences of this restless pace—which again is connected with the entire structure and functionality of the advanced industrial society—are, precisely, stress. Thus the various yoga and meditation techniques that are included in both the youth religions (yes, the young are under stress in school!) and the body-religions seem clearly aimed at counteracting the futuristic orientation and its consequent stress. "Inner peace" is one of the designations for the result of meditation or meditative experience. About the yoga of "Kundalini," it is said:

> The *kundalini* [*urkraft,* original power, JG-M] moves up through the body and works its way through all the psychophysical tensions and resistances it meets on its way. "In its ascent," says Sanella [apparently an American physician], "the *kundalini* has the effect that the central nervous system is freed from stress. The regions of stress will usually cause pain during meditation. When the *kundalini* meets these stress regions or blockages, it begins, by itself, to work; it goes ahead with a self-steered and self-regulated process whereby it spreads throughout the psycho-physical system in order to remove these blockages. (Sathyarthi 1982, 2, 282)

Another quite obvious reason for the flourishing of body religions at present may be described as scepsis in relation to modern medical science. I believe we can point to two things here: one has to do with what within medical ethics is discussed under the heading of "paternalism." That is to say, physicians are prone, both by tradition and training, to behave like authorities (*patres*) whose evaluations and decisions cannot and must not be discussed (cf. Glebe-Möller 1980b, 128ff.). For the younger members of the middle class, those brought up to take positions and make decisions for themselves, it is naturally intolerable to be subjected to the physician's authoritative paternalism. The body-therapeutic literature, on the other hand, aimed to a large degree at self-study, hits the problem head-on. It gives—or at least purports to give—the reader and user the possibility of determining for himself or herself what methods of treatment are best suited to him or her.

The second thing is connected with certain characteristic features in the content of medical education today—and with which modern medicine, especially Western medicine, has become synonymous, namely, the enormous utilization of chemical preparations ("pills") and of all forms of technology. Both are reflected in the predominant natural-science orientation of the education that physicians receive (cf. Jacobsen 1982). What can be concluded from this—at least on a certain intellectual level—is that the pills do not help, and that the widespread use of medical technology does not stand to measure with the results obtained. It is typical that the body religions, regardless of the therapeutic format in which they appear, demand neither chemical substances nor technology.

As a direct parallel to traditional medical treatment appears something generally designated as *healing*. Healing comes in many variations, and is a widespread form of treatment in the Anglo-Saxon world—in England, for example, it is recognized by the state's department of health. Healing is primarily a matter of touch—the healer, by laying hands on the patient, can induce a condition of relaxation and thus relieve stress and pain. Although charlatans naturally have rich possibilities here, it seems a fundamentally sound practice—in harmony even with Jesus' healing praxis—to put emphasis on physical contact between human beings. In the final analysis, neither words nor pills can make sick people well!

A third reason for the flourishing of body religions has to do with the rising awareness of the significance of milieu, environment, and nutrition for the physical and psychical well-being of humans. "Health medicine" fads of every description are closely connected with the body religions. The market for health products and literature about them coincides for the most part with the body religion market—and runs clear over into the "green" ecological-political movements. A book concerning the spectrum I am referring to here is entitled *Strategy for a Better Life.* This title could also sum up the stated goals of the more exotic body religions. More or less explicitly, what is expressed here is an opposition to industrial society, as it has developed, where growth and profit are held in the highest regard without consideration for the consequences for milieu or body. Characteristic of most of this opposition, however, is that there is little or no reflection as to *why* growth and profit dominate. And consequently, there are few if any conscious attempts made to get at the fundamental causes. One remains on the level of narcissism and rejects outright that there should be a *political* way to a better life. The author of *The Ways of the Body* expresses this in characteristic terms:

> Alterations in the outer conditions alone will not, as far as I can see, bring real inner (or outer) liberation—something the 20th century's social-revolutionary activities point out. Only by bringing about the individual's liberation from the yokes of the past and from personal egotism does it seem possible to work constructively, in common, to bring about living conditions worthy of humanity. (Sathyarthi 1982, 121)

It is precisely this individualism/narcissism that makes it impossible to build a bridge between the youth and body religions, on the one hand, and the praxis of the Christian church or community, on the other. There is clearly a new awakening of religious interest here—in this respect, the secularization thesis has been disproved by the facts—but this interest is characterized by ignoring the crucifixion. And it is in the crucifixion, in suffering, that solidarity with others who suffer shows itself. Where this solidarity does not exist, Christian praxis is not found. So, in my view, according to the interpretation of the Jesus-figure which I have presented here, nothing can Christianly be built on the new religiosity. It would be better to go to the various "grass-roots" movements: the pensioners movement, the women's movement, the peace movement, the decent housing movement, "the christianites," "the slum stormers," and so forth, even though they in no way decorate themselves with religious feathers. For the paradox is—or is it really all that paradoxical?—that those who most strongly appeal to the theological code are perhaps in actual fact the farthest removed from the Jesus story. And those who would not dream of appealing to or claiming Jesus stand the closest to the actant Jesus. Strangely enough, provisions are actually made for this paradox (if it is a paradox) in the Jesus narrative:

> When the Son of man comes in his glory, and all the angels with him, then he will sit on his glorious throne. Before him will be gathered all the nations, and he will separate them one from another as a shepherd separates the sheep from the goats, and he will place the sheep at his right hand, but the goats at his left. Then the King will say to those at his right hand, "Come, O blessed of my Father, inherit the kingdom prepared for you from the foundation of the world; for I was hungry and you gave me food, I was thirsty and you gave me drink, I was a stranger and you welcomed me, I was naked and you clothed me, I was sick and you visited me, I was in prison and you came to me." Then the righteous will answer him, "Lord, when did we see thee hungry and feed thee, or thirsty and give thee drink? And when did we see thee a stranger and welcome thee, or naked and clothe thee? And when did we see thee sick or in prison and visit thee?" And the King will answer them, "Truly, I say to you, as you did it to one of the least of these my brethren, you did it to me." Then he will say to those at his left hand, "Depart from me, you cursed, into the eternal fire prepared for the devil and his angels; for I was hungry and you gave me no food, I was thirsty and you gave me no drink, I was a stranger and you did not welcome me, naked and you did not clothe me, sick and in prison and you did not visit me." Then they also will answer, "Lord, when did we see thee hungry or thirsty or a stranger or naked or sick or in prison, and did not minister to thee?" Then he will answer them, "Truly I say to you, as you did it not to one of the least of these, you did it not

to me." And they will go away into eternal punishment, but the righteous into eternal life. (Matt. 25:31–46)

Notes

1. Against the thesis concerning the correlation of modernity and secularity, a critic such as Mary Douglas has noted that even before modernity there were people "in many times and places" that found it possible to live their lives without benefit of the integrating functions of religion (cf. Douglas 1982). This objection, in my opinion, at most impacts Weber's or Habermas's reconstruction of the historical developments in religion, not their description of the function of religion within modernity.

BIBLIOGRAPHY

Augustine of Hippo

1953 *Confessions.* Vol. 21 of Fathers of the Church. Washington, D.C.: Catholic University of America Press.

Baillie, D. M.

1948 *God Was in Christ.* London: Faber & Faber.

Baum, Gregory

1981 n.t. In *Signs of the Time.* Edited by Norman Vale. Toronto.

1981a n.t. In *Neo-Conservatism: Social and Religious Phenomenon.* Concilium 141. Edited by Gregory Baum et. al. New York: Harper & Row.

Belo, Fernando

1976 *Lecture materialiste de l'evangile de Marc: Recit-Practique-Ideologie.* 3d ed. Paris: Cerf.

1981 *A Materialist Reading of the Gospel of Mark.* Translated by Matthew J. O'Connel. Maryknoll, N.Y.: Orbis Books.

Berger, Peter L.

1967 *The Sacred Canopy.* Garden City, N.Y.: Doubleday & Co.

Bloch, Ernst

1970 *Atheismus und Christentum.* Reinbek bei Hamburg: Rowohlt.

1972 *Atheism in Christianity.* Translated by J. T. Swann. New York: Herder & Herder.

Boesak, Allan

1977 *Farewell to Innocence: A Socio-Ethical Study of Black Theology and Power.* Maryknoll, N.Y.: Orbis Books.

Boff, Leonardo

1983 *The Lord's Prayer: The Prayer of Integral Liberation.* Maryknoll, N.Y.: Orbis Books.

Bonhoeffer, Dietrich

1966 *Widerstand und Ergebung.* Munich. Chr. Kaiser Verlag.

1972 *Letters and Papers from Prison.* Translated and edited by Eberhard Bethge. New York: Macmillan Co.

Bouyer, Louis et. al.

1963 *History of Christian Spirituality.* Vol. 1, *The Spirituality of the New Testament and the Fathers.* New York: Seabury Press, 1982.

Brueggemann, Walter

1978 *The Prophetic Imagination.* Philadelphia: Fortress Press.

Bugenhagen, Johannes

1888 n.t. In *Dr. Johannes Bugenhagens Briefwechsel.* Edited by O. Vogt. Stettin: Saunier.

Bultmann, Rudolf

1951 *Jesus.* Tübingen: J. C. B. Mohr (Paul Siebeck).

1958 *Jesus and the Word.* Translated by Louise P. Smith and Erminie H. Lantero. New York: Charles Scribner's Sons.

1968 *The History of the Synoptic Tradition.* Rev. ed. New York: Harper & Row.

1970 *Geschichte der synoptischen Tradition.* 8th ed. Göttingen: Vandenhoek S Ruprecht.

Burke, Peter

1978 *Popular Culture in Early Modern Europe.* London: UKE.

Bynum, Caroline Walker

1982 *Jesus as Mother: Studies in the Spirituality of the High Middle Ages.* Berkeley: University of California Press.

Casperz, Paul

1979 "Jesus of Nazareth and Human Understanding." In *Living Theology in Asia.* Edited by Paul C. England. London: SCM Press.

Casserley, J. V. Langmead

1961 *The Christian in Philosophy.* New York.

Chagnon, Roland
1979 *Les Charismatiques au Quebec*. Montreal: Quebec/ Amerique.

Christ, Carol P.
1980 *Diving Deep and Surfacing: Women Writers on Spiritual Quest*. Boston: Beacon Press.

Collins, Sheila D.
1975 *A Different Heaven and Earth*. Valley Forge, Pa.

Cone, James S.
1975 *God of the Oppressed*. New York: Harper & Row.

Crosby, Michael H.
1977 *Thy Will Be Done: Praying the Our Father as Subversive Activity*. Maryknoll, N.Y.: Orbis Books.

Daly, Mary
1973 *Beyond God the Father: Towards a Philosophy of Women's Liberation*. Boston: Beacon Press.
1978 *Gyn/Ecology: The Metaethics of Radical Feminism*. Boston: Beacon Press.

Davis, Charles
1976 *Body as Spirit: The Nature of Religious Feelings*. New York: Seabury Press.
1982 "The Theological Career of Historical Criticism of the Bible." *Cross Currents* 32/3.

Den danske Salmebog
n.d. n.p.

de Santa Ana, Julio, ed.
1979 *Towards a Church of the Poor*. Geneva: The World Council of Churches. U.S. edition. Maryknoll, New York: Orbis Books, 1981.

Douglas, Mary
1982 "The Effects of Modernization on Religious Change." *Daedalus*, 111/1 (1982). 1–19.

Ebbestad Hansen, Jan-Erik
1978 "Jacob Bohme: Liv—tenkning—historiske forutsetninger." Ph.D. diss., Oslo University.

Fischer, Joseph A. ed.
1956 *Die apostolischen Vater*. Munich.

Forum for kvindeforskning
1983 "The New Spirituality." 1.

Franz, Günther

1963 *Quellen zur Geschichte des Bauernkrieges.* Munich: R. Oldenbourg.

Friis, Henning

1981 *Nederst ved bordet: En rapport om fattigdom og fattigdomspolitik i Danmark.* Copenhagen: Socialforskningsinstituttet.

Frostin, Per

1983 n.t. In *Fred og Nedrustning—Kirkens ansvar?.* Edited by Peder Nörgaard-Höjen. Aarhus: Anis.

Frye, Northrop

1982 *The Great Code: The Bible and Literature.* London. New York: Harcourt Brace Jovanovich, 1983.

Gadamer, Hans-Georg

1965 *Wahrheit und Methode.* 2nd ed. Tübingen: J.C.B. Mohr (Paul Siebeck).

1975 *Truth and Method.* Translated and edited by Garret Barden and John Cumming. New York: Seabury Press.

Girard, Rene

1977 *Violence and the Sacred.* Translated by Patrick Gregory. Baltimore: Johns Hopkins University Press.

1980 *La violence et la sacre.* Paris.

Gjesing, Lars Ole

1980 "Den materialistiske eksegese og hermeneutikken." *Dansk Teologisk Tidsskrift,* 2.

Glebe-Möller, Jens

1979 "Socialetiske aspekter i Niels Hemmingsens forfatterskab." *Kirkehistoriske Samlinger.*

1980 *Det teologiske fakultet 1597–1732.* Vol. 5 of *Köbenhavns Universitets Historie 1479–1979.* Edited by Leif Grane et. al. Copenhagen: Köbenhavns Universitet.

1980a "The Good Samaritan in Recent American Moral Philosophy." *Danish Yearbook of Philosophy,* 17.

1980b *Om moralen.* Copenhagen: Gad.

1982 "K.E. Lögstrup: En Ny Marx?" *Præsteforeningens Blad,* 45.

1983 "Replique." *Fönix,* 2.

1983a (Discussion with Jörgen I. Jensen.) *Kredsen,* 3, 4.

1983b "Filosofi og religion." *Præsteforeningens Blad,* 11.

1987 *A Political Dogmatic.* Philadelphia: Fortress Press.

Gottwald, Norman K.

1980 *The Tribes of Yahweh: A Sociology of the Religion of Liberated Israel.* London: SCM Press.

Grane, Leif

1968 *Protest og konsekvens: Faser i Martin Luthers tænkning indtil 1525.* Copenhagen.

Grane, Leif, et. al, eds.

1980 *Köbenhavns Universitets Historie 1479–1979.* Copenhagen: Köbenhavns Universitet.

Grillmeier, A.

1965 *Christ in Christian Tradition.* Translated and expanded by J. S. Bowden. New York: Sheed and Ward.

Grillmeier, A., and Bacht, H., eds.

1962 *Das Konzil von Chalcedon.* Vol. 1–2. Wurtzburg: Echter-Verlag.

Grundtvig, N. F. S.

1944 *Grundtvigs Sangværk.* Vol. 1. Copenhagen: Det danske forlag.

1906 *Udvalgte skrifter.* Vol. 4. Copenhagen: Gyldendal.

Gutierrez, Gustavo

1973 *A Theology of Liberation.* Maryknoll, N.Y.: Orbis Books.

Haack, Friedrich-Wilhelm

1981 *Jugendreligionen: Ursachen—Trends—Reaktionen.* Munich: Claudins Verlag.

Haahr, Erik, and Haas Pedersen, Tove, trans.

1983 *Uvidenhedens sky—hvori sjelen bliver et med Gud.* Copenhagen: Borgen.

Habermas, Jürgen

1981 *Theorie des kommunikative Handels.* Vols. 1–2. Frankfurt: Suhrkamp.

1984, 1987 *The Theory of Communicative Action.* Translated by Thomas McCarthy. Boston: Beacon Press.

Hallbäck, Geert

1982 "Materialistische Exegese und strukturale Analyse." *Linguistica Biblica,* 50.

1983 *Strukturalisme og eksegese.* Copenhagen: Gad.

Hartnack, Justus
1980 *Menneskerettigheder*. Haarby: Forlaget i Haarby.

Hauerwas, Stanley
1981 *A Community of Character: Towards a Constructive Christian Social Ethic*. Notre Dame, Ind.: University of Notre Dame Press.

Haughton, Rosemary
1981 *The Passionate God*. New York: Paulist Press.

Helgesen, Paul
1932 *Skrifter*. Vol. 1. Copenhagen: Gydendal.

Hellesnes, Jon
n.d. "Ironi og livssyn." Mimeographed manuscript. Tromsö: n.p.

Hengel, Martin
1977 *Crucifixion*. Philadelphia: Fortress Press.

Henry, Patrick
1979 *New Directions in New Testament Study*. Philadelphia: Westminster Press.

Herzel, Susannah
1978 n.t. In *Man, Woman, Priesthood*. Edited by Peter Moore. London: SPCK.
1981 *A Voice for Women*. Geneva: World Council of Churches.

Hoffmann, Manfred
1983 "Latinamerikansk befrielsesteologi sedd i ett skandinaviskt sammanhang." Unpublished lecture manuscript.

Höjrup, Thomas
1983 *Det glemte folk*. Copenhagen: Statens Bygetorskningsinstitut.

Holm, Sören
1955 *Religionsfilosofi*. Copenhagen: Nyt Nordisk Forlag Arnold Busck.

Holmer, Paul
1979 n.t. In *Black Theology: A Documentary History, 1966–1979*. Edited by Gayraud S. Wilmore and James S. Cone. Maryknoll, N.Y.: Orbis Books.

Holmquist and Nörregaard
1949 *Kirkehistorie*. Vol. 2. 3d. ed. Copenhagen: Schultz.

Hunter, A. M.
1973 *The Work and Words of Jesus*. Rev. ed. London: Westminster Press.

Ignatius of Loyola
1881 *Manresa: Or the Spiritual Exercises of St. Ignatius.* London: Burns & Oates.

Illeris, et. al.
1982 *Ungdomspsykologi: Samfundssituationen. Handlemönstre. Bevisthedsformer.* Copenhagen: Unge pädagoger.

Iversen, Hans
1982 *Tro, Håb or Kærlighet. Sækulariseringen og socialisation grundtvigsk forstået.* Aarhus: Anis.

Jacobsen, Bo
1982 *De höjere utdannelser mellom teknologi og humanisme.* Copenhagen: Rhodos.

Jensen, Jörgen I.
1983 (Discussion with Jens Glebe-Möller.) *Kredsen,* 3, 4.

Jensen, Ole
1983 n.t. In *Fred og nedrustning—kirkens ansvar?* Edited by Peder Nörgaard-Höjen. Aarhus: Anis.

Jervell, Jakob
1972 *Luke and the People of God.* Minneapolis: Augsburg Publishing House.

Jörgensen, Theodor
1983 "Review." *Fönix,* 1.

Karris, Robert J.
1978 "Poor and Rich: The Lukan Sitz im Leben." In *Perspectives on Luke–Acts.* Edited by Charles H. Talbert. Danville: NABPR (Mercer Press).

Käsemann, Ernst
1965 "Das Problem des historischen Jesus." In *Exegetische Versuche und Besinnungen.* 4th ed. Göttingen: Vandenhock & Ruprecht.

1968 "The Problem of the Historical Jesus." In *Essays on New Testament Themes.* Translated by W. J. Montague. London: SCM Press.

Kavanaugh, John Francis
1981 *Following Christ in a Consumer Society: The Spirituality of Cultural Resistance.* Maryknoll, N.Y.: Orbis Books.

Kee, Howard Clark
1977 *Community of the New Age: Studies in Mark's Gospel.* Philadelphia: Westminster Press.

Kemp, Peter
1973 *Poetique de l'engagement.* Paris: Le Seuil.

Kermode, Frank
1979 *The Genesis of Secrecy: On the Interpretation of Narrative.* Cambridge: Harvard University Press.

Kierkegaard, Sören (Anti-Climacus)
1963 *Indövelse i Christendom.* [*Samlede Vaerker.* Vol. 16. 3d ed.] Copenhagen: Gyldendal.

Kinnamon, Michael
1982 "Asian Theology and the Ecumenical Movement." Unpublished lecture manuscript.

Kiselberg, Steffen, and Glebe-Möller, Jens, eds.
1982 *Tidens problem.* Copenhagen: Gyldendal.

Kohlberg, Lawrence, and Power, Clark
1981 "Moral Development, Religious Thinking, and the Question of a Seventh Stage." *Zygon* 16:3.

Küng, Hans
1970 *Menschwerdung Gottes.* Freiburg: Herder.
1987 *The Incarnation of God.* Translated by J. R. Stephenson. New York: Crossroad.

Kysar, Robert
1975 *The Fourth Evangelist and his Gospel: An Examination of Contemporary Scholarship.* Minneapolis: Augsburg Publishing House.

Lasch, Christopher
1979 *The Culture of Narcissism.* New York: Warner Books.

Larsen, Ejvind
1983 *Det levende ord: Om Grundtvig.* Copenhagen: Rosinante.

Léger, Danièle
1982 "Apocalyptique ecologie et 'retour' de la religion." *Archives de sciences sociales des religions,* 53, 1.

Lemche, Niels Peter
1982 Review of *A Political Dogmatic,* by Jens Glebe-Möller. *Dansk Teologisk Tidsskrift,* 1.

Lindhardt, Jan
1983 *Martin Luthers erkendelse og formidling in renæssancen.* Copenhagen: Borgen.

Lögstrup, K. E.
1978 *Skabelse og tilintetgjörelse.* Copenhagen: Gyldendal.

Lonergan, Bernard
1972 *Method in Theology.* New York: Harper & Row.

Lundager Jensen, Hans Jörn
1980 "Diesseits und Jenseits des Raumes eines Textes." *Linguistica Biblica* 47.

Luther, Martin
1967 *Luther's Works.* Volume 46, *The Christian in Society, 3.* Edited by Robert C. Schultz. Philadelphia: Fortress Press.
1978 "The Freedom of a Christian." In *Three Treatises.* From the American edition of *Luther's Works.* Philadelphia: Fortress Press.

MacIntyre, Alasdair
1981 *After Virtue: A Study of Moral Theology.* Notre Dame, Ind.: University of Notre Dame Press.

Marshall, I. Howard
1978 *The Gospel of Luke.* Grand Rapids: Wm. B. Eerdmans.

Martyn, J. Louis
1968 *History and Theology in the Fourth Gospel.* New York: Harper & Row.
1978 *The Gospel of John in Christian History: Essays for Interpreters.* Paramus, N. J.: Paulist Press.

Marx, Karl, and Engels, Friedrich
1959 *Basic Writings on Politics and Philosophy.* Edited by Lewis S. Feuer. Garden City, N.Y.: Doubleday Anchor Books.

Metz, Johann Baptist
1977 *Glaube in Geschichte und Gesellschaft.* Mainz: Matthias-Grünewald.
1980 *Faith in History and Society.* Translated by David Smith. New York: Seabury Press.

Meyer, Ben F.
1979 *The Aims of Jesus.* London: SCM Press.

Miranda, José
1977 *Being and Messiah: The Message of St. John.* Maryknoll, N.Y.: Orbis Books.

Moore, Sebastian
1980 *The Fire and the Rose Are One.* New York: Harper & Row.

New Hymnbook for North-American Unitarians
n.d.

Nielsen, Erik A.
1981 In *Fönix,* 4.
1982 In *Fönix,* 4.

Nietzsche, Friedrich
1921 *Vom Nutzen und Nachteil der Historie für das Leben.* Vol. 2. Stuttgart: Kröner Verlag.
1921a *Der Antichrist.* Vol. 35. Stuttgart: Kröner Verlag.

Nordentoft, Kresten
1973 *Hvad siger Brand-Majoren? Kierkegaards opgör med sin Samtid.* Coppenhagen: Gad.

Nozick, Robert
1974 *Anarchy, State and Utopia.* New York: Basic Books.

Pagels, Elaine
1979 *The Gnostic Gospels.* New York: Random House.

Patte, Daniel et. al.
1978 *Structural Exegesis: From Theory to Practice.* Philadelphia: Fortress Press.

Pieris, Aloysius
1979 "The Asian Sense in Theology." In *Living Theology in Asia.* Edited by John C. England. London: SCM Press.

Pobee, John S.
1979 *Toward an African Theology.* Nashville: Abingdon Press.

Poulton, John
1982 *The Feast of Life.* Geneva: World Council of Churches.

Prenter, Regin
1955 *Skabelse og genlösning.* 2d ed. Copenhagen: Gad.

Rapp, Francis
1975 "Die soziale und wirtschaftliche Vorgeschichte des Bauernkriges im Unterelsass." In *Schriften des Vereins fur Reformationsgeschichte,* 189. Gütersloh: Gütersloher Verlaghaus.

Rawls, John
1971 *A Theory of Justice.* Cambridge: Harvard University Press.

Ruether, Rosemary
1983 *Sexism and God-Talk: Toward a Feminist Theology.* Boston: Beacon Press.

Sathyarthi, Swami Deva
1982 *Kroppens veje,* 1–2. Copenhagen: Borgen.

Schillebeeckx, Edward
1977 *Christus und die Christen: Die Geschichte einer neuen Lebenspraxis.* Freiburg/Basel/Wien.
1980 *Christ: The Experience of Jesus as Lord.* Translated by John Bowden. New York: Seabury Press.

Schweizer, Eduard
1980 *Luke: A Challenge to Present Theology*. Atlanta: John Knox Press.

Seiffert, Helmut
1973 *Einfuhrung in die Wissenschaftstheorie,* 2. 5th ed. Munich: C.H. Beck.

Semeia Decatur, Ga.: Scholars Press.

Sjörup, Lene
1981 "(Nogle) kvinders religiöse oplevelser." *Kritisk forum for praktisk teologi,* 7.
1983 In *Forum for kvindeforskning,* 1.

Slök, Johannes
1981 *Det religiöse sprog*. Aarhus: Centrum.

Sobrino, Jon
1978 *Christology at the Crossroads*. Maryknoll, N. Y.: Orbis Books.

Sölle, Dorothee
1973 *Leiden*. Stuttgart: Kreutz Verlag.

Song, Choan-Seng
1979 *Third-Eye Theology*. Maryknoll, N.Y.: Orbis Books.
1981 *The Tears of Lady Meng: A Parable of People's Political Theology*. Geneva: World Council of Churches. U.S. edition. Maryknoll, N. Y.: Orbis Books.

Starhawk
1978 *Dreaming the Dark, Magic, Sex, and Politics*. Boston: Beacon Press.

Starobinsky, Jean
1971 In *Analyse structurale et exegese biblique*. Edited by R. Barthes et. al. Neuchatel: Delachaux & Niestlé.

Tausen, Hans
1870 (Against Jens Beldebak.) In *Smaaskrifter af Hans Tausen*. Edited by H. F. Rördam. Copenhagen: Det Kgl. danske Selskab.

Theissen, Gerd
1979 *Jesusoverleveringen og dens sociale baggrund*. Copenhagen: Hans Reitzel.

van Dulmen, R.
1977 *Reformation als Revolution*. Munich: DTV.

Vogels, Walter
1980 "Les limites de la methode historico-critique." *Laval Theologique Philosophique* (June).

Værge, Johs.

1974 *Jesus-bevaegelsen: En oversigt over amerikanske og danske grupperinger—En analyse av tekster.* Mimeographed. Aarhus: Aarhus University.

n.d. "Danish Jesus-Groups 1969–75." Manuscript.

Weber, Max

1970 *Gesammelte Aufsätze zur Religionssoziologie, I.* 6th ed. Tübingen: J.C.B. Mohr (Paul Siebeck).

Zschäbitz, G.

1967 *Martin Luther: Grösse und Grenze.* Berlin: Dentscher Verlag der Wissenschaften.

Index of Names